THE PICTORIAL HISTORY OF
KNIVES
DAGGERS & BAYONETS

A CHRONOLOGY OF SHARP-EDGED WEAPONS AND BLADES FROM AROUND THE WORLD, WITH OVER 225 PHOTOGRAPHS AND ILLUSTRATIONS

DR TOBIAS CAPWELL

This edition is published by Southwater,
an imprint of Anness Publishing Ltd,
Hermes House, 88–89 Blackfriars Road,
London SE1 8HA; tel. 020 7401 2077; fax 020 7633 9499
www.southwaterbooks.com; www.annesspublishing.com

Anness Publishing has a new picture agency outlet for images for
publishing, promotions or advertising. Please visit our website
www.practicalpictures.com for more information.

UK distributor: Book Trade Services;
tel. 0116 2759086; fax 0116 2759090;
uksales@booktradeservices.com; exportsales@booktradeservices.com
North American distributor: National Book Network;
tel. 301 459 3366; fax 301 429 5746; www.nbnbooks.com
Australian distributor: Pan Macmillan Australia;
tel. 1300 135 113; fax 1300 135 103; customer.service@macmillan.com.au
New Zealand distributor: David Bateman Ltd;
tel. (09) 415 7664; fax (09) 415 8892

Publisher: Joanna Lorenz
Project Editors: Sarah Doughty, Hazel Songhurst and Dan Hurst
Photography: Gary Ombler and David Cummings
Designer: Alistair Plumb
Proofreading Manager: Lindsay Zamponi
Production Controller: Wendy Lawson

Designed and prduced for Anness Publishing by
THE BRIDGEWATER BOOK COMPANY LTD

ETHICAL TRADING POLICY
At Anness Publishing we believe that business should be conducted in
an ethical and ecologically sustainable way, with respect for the
environment and a proper regard to the replacement of the natural
resources we employ.

As a publisher, we use a lot of wood pulp in high-quality paper for
printing, and that wood commonly comes from spruce trees. We are
therefore currently growing more than 750,000 trees in three Scottish
forest plantations: Berrymoss (130 hectares/320 acres), West Touxhill
(125 hectares/305 acres) and Deveron Forest (75 hectares/185 acres).
The forests we manage contain more than 3.5 times the number of trees
employed each year in making paper for the books we manufacture.

Because of this ongoing ecological investment programme, you, as
our customer, can have the pleasure and reassurance of knowing that a
tree is being cultivated on your behalf to naturally replace the materials
used to make the book you are holding.

Our forestry programme is run in accordance with the UK Woodland
Assurance Scheme (UKWAS) and will be certified by the internationally
recognized Forest Stewardship Council (FSC). The FSC is a non-
government organization dedicated to promoting responsible
management of the world's forests. Certification ensures forests are
managed in an environmentally sustainable and socially responsible way.
For further information about this scheme, go to
www.annesspublishing.com/trees

Previously published as part of a larger volume, *The Illustrated
Encyclopedia of Knives, Daggers and Bayonets*

PUBLISHER'S NOTE
Although the advice and information in this book are believed to be
accurate and true at the time of going to press, neither the authors nor
the publisher can accept any legal responsibility or liability for any errors
or omissions that may be made.

PICTURE CREDITS
The publisher would like to thank the following for kindly supplying photos
for this book: AKG: 5t, 8l, r, 11t, 13t, 14t, 15t, 16t, 17bl, 18tl, 19t, b, 20bl, 27r,
28r, l, 29tr, 32b, 34r, 35br, 36t, 49bl, t, 50bl, 51tl, 53t, 56t, 58tr, 59t, 60b, 69t,
75br, 77tr, 86bl, br, 89t, b, 92tl, 93b; Alamy: 7br, 26b, 35t, 10t, 65t, 76tl, 81tr;
Ancient Art & Architecture: 15b; Berman Museum of World History,
Alabama: 4mt, 53b, 55t, 61b, 65b, 73b; Bridgeman Art Library: 4b, 9tr, b,
10b, 11b, 12t, 14b, 17t, 18tr, 22b, 25bl, 26mt, 30b, 31tr, 34l, 38b, 39t, 43t,
47ml, 55b, 57br, 63bl, 70tl, 76br, 83t; Bruun-rasmussen: 7tl Corbis: 54tl, tr,
61t, 67t, 75tr; Furrer, Richard 94b; Getty Images: 64b, 66b; Hermann
Historica Auctioneers, Munich: 5b, 6t, 17br, 18b, 21b, 29bb, 31b, 38mr, 39b,
42t, 46b, 47r, 52t, 77tl, 79t, mt, 81b, 82b, 83 m, tb, bb, 85tr, 85bl, 87tl, tm,
88tm, 90t, 91br, 92bm; photos.com: 41tr; Picture Desk: 71tl; Topfoto: 6bb,
tb, 11mr, 12b, 16b, 20t, 23r, 33b, 44b, 45bl, 62t, 69br, 72b, 73t, 74tt, mt, 78tr,
91t; Wallis and Wallis Auction Gallery: 70br, 71tr; Werner Forman Picture
Library: 42b. All other images from the Royal Armouries, Leeds in England.
All artwork by Peters & Zabransky Ltd.

Every effort has been made to obtain permission to reproduce copyright
material, but there may be cases where we have been unable to trace a
copyright holder. The publisher will be happy to correct any omissions in
future printings.

Contents

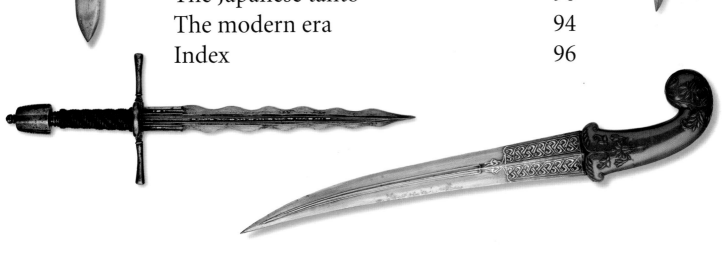

Introduction

From the sharp flints with which primitive humans defended themselves to the carbon-steel bayonets carried by modern soldiers, the fighting knife's history is a complex tale of technical ingenuity, artistic virtuosity and brutal violence. Like its larger cousin the sword, this lethal edged weapon expressed the wealth and taste of its owner. But it was also a vital last resort – easy to carry, quick to draw and always at the fighting man's side.

Butt cap

Spacer

Strong stabbing point

Early daggers and fighting knives

Our story begins well over a million years ago. The earliest sharpened tools were fashioned by knapping flints into sharp shapes. Around 8,000 years ago, copper was first worked in Asia. Four millennia later, alloyed metals were developed. Bronze remained the mainstay of technology until iron became available 2,000 years later. Iron was being produced in large quantities by Roman times, when soldiers were armed with the feared pugio dagger and gladius sword. Just as iconic was the single-edged scramasax of central European peoples.

Medieval and Renaissance daggers

The daggers of the first medieval knights were probably similar to small Viking and Saxon handsaxes. Like the knight's sword, these daggers acquired cruciform hilts and often double-edged blades. As armour became more effective, more specialized medieval daggers evolved to defeat it. New hilt types gave a better grip, while blades were narrowed into sharp triangular or square-sectioned spikes.

From before the 11th until after the 16th century, the dagger was an essential battlefield weapon. It was also carried in civilian life for self-defence because, until the 16th century, swords were not worn with everyday dress. When the long, heavy-bladed civilian

ABOVE Highland dress dirk, Scottish, *c.*1868. The word "dirk" is usually applied to the long fighting knife of the Scottish Highlanders – of which this is a late example – and to certain classes of military dress dagger.

RIGHT King Henry VIII (1491–1547) is portrayed in this portrait by Holbein wearing a gilded dagger as part of his courtly dress. The dagger was an essential fashion accessory for medieval and Renaissance men.

rapier came into fashion, the dagger became its parrying aid. But by the early 1600s sword blades were lighter and could be used rapidly to attack and defend. The parrying dagger was discarded, and daggers declined as fashion accessories. Characteristic forms were worn only in certain rural areas, like the long dirks in the Scottish Highlands and the western Mediterranean.

Bayonets from the 17th to the 21st century

Just as the dagger was falling out of favour, it found a new role: the dagger became the bayonet.

The earliest Bayonne daggers were probably not bayonets at all but rather ordinary daggers made in southwestern France. In order to transform a musket into a spear for close-quarters combat, soldiers started jamming daggers into the muzzles of weapons. The plug bayonet was born – a short-lived design, since it was impossible to fire the weapon with the bayonet in place. This was replaced by the socket bayonet, which became the standard issue.

Mechanized warfare in the 19th century meant that fighting forces became more diversified. One consequence was more varieties of bayonet, including unwieldy sword bayonets that, though impractical, remained in use through the 1800s. By the 20th century bayonets had begun to revert to their dagger-like origins; most soldiers now carry some form of knife bayonet, which is both an all-purpose tool and a weapon.

Daggers in Asia and Africa

In Africa fighting knives and daggers assumed exotic, uniquely creative forms. Although important as weapons, many were also status symbols and forms of currency. Turning east, we encounter the dagger culture of the Middle East, where the Arab jambiya remains an essential part of formal male dress, and

features in celebrations. We continue into Persia, which produced very skilled bladesmiths, masters of the art of "watered" or wootz steel. Fine Persian daggers are often superlative jewellery objects, rivalled only by the work of the Mughals from northern India.

In the Far East, the Japanese produced the fabulous tanto and aikuchi, smaller companions of the fabled katana sword of the samurai. Finally, our journey ends in the South Pacific with the Indonesian kris, prized by European collectors since the 17th century, purported to have magical powers, and still felt to embody the spirit of the region.

About this book

This fascinating history traces the fighting blade from the earliest sharpened flints of prehistory to the survival knives and hardened steel bayonets of modern combat. Used by ancient warriors, medieval knights and soldiers of the American Civil War and the two World Wars, knives, daggers and bayonets have helped shape human history and are symbols of power, survival and progress.

BELOW Ottoman Turkish knife, 17th century. The finest Persian and Turkish daggers were usually forged of watered steel – giving strength and elasticity to the blade – and fitted with jade, ivory or crystal hilts.

Watered steel blade
from Persia or India

Jade hilt from Turkey

The earliest knives

The first weapons invented by humans were made out of the materials that they could pick up off the ground or extract from the bodies of the animals they killed for food. They shaped and sharpened wood, horn and bone for many different uses. They could throw rocks and use them to deal lethal blows. The right sorts of rocks could also be fashioned into extremely sharp cutting tools.

LEFT This late Neolithic flint knife (*c.*2000BC) was found in Jutland, Denmark. Flint flakes have been carefully and skilfully removed to form the sharp blade and tapered grip.

Compared with the most ancient edged implements, the fighting knife and dagger are fairly recent advances. The ancestors of modern humans first began to fashion sharpened objects out of stone about a million years ago. But these early cutting devices were made with a number of utilitarian purposes in mind. Perhaps they could have been used in a fight if the need arose, but there is no evidence to suggest that this was their primary function. Instead, these sharpened stones were mainly used for shaping wooden tools, butchering animals and scraping hides clean before making them into clothes.

The first weapons

The earliest stone tools were not very effective weapons because they were small and did not increase the reach of the user. Neither could they be used to stab, for most had no significant points. The hand axes in use up until around 35,000BC were roughly teardrop-shaped, with a rudimentary point, but these cannot be considered stabbing weapons. As weapons, these axes could have had no more specialist usefulness than any other naturally sharp rock.

For a hand weapon to be considered a fighting knife or dagger, it must increase or alter the user's reach to some advantageous extent, and it must provide the ability to stab. Cutting is in many cases another useful property, but it is secondary in the case of weapons under about 20cm (8in) in length. Stone is a very brittle and weighty material, and could not be used to create weapons with long cutting edges. A stone sword would have been excessively heavy and broken at the first blow. Nonetheless towards the end of the Middle Stone Age (*c.*50,000 years ago), early humans, aided by good stone-working techniques, were able to make short, sharply pointed stabbing knives.

BELOW The design of this Native American antler knife has changed little in 4000 years.

BOTTOM A Bronze Age knife, carved in bone, copies the form of copper knives of the time.

Polished elk antler

Curved bone blade

Wrist thong

ABOVE This group of flint knives of the late Stone Age and Bronze Age shows a degree of variety but also key similarities. The blades must remain short and stout, or they would simply break.

Stone and metal weapons

The use of stone knives did not end suddenly with the discovery of metals around 3500BC. Indeed, most of the finest surviving stone knives and daggers were made as recently as 2000 years into the Bronze Age (c.3500–c.700BC). In some places, metal knives seem to have influenced the form of stone ones; for example, stone daggers found in Scandinavia dating from around 1600BC appear to be direct copies of their metal counterparts. This is probably because early metalworking was well under way around the Mediterranean long before it appeared in northern Europe. Metal daggers from the south may have found their way north, where their forms were copied using local materials. The height of this period of technological crossover, roughly 1800–1500BC, is often referred to as the "Dagger Period" because knives and daggers were clearly enormously popular during this time.

Flint knapping

The process by which a hard stone, such as flint, quartzite or obsidian (a vitreous acid volcanic rock) is reduced to a specific shape for use as a tool or weapon is called flint knapping. Along with the ability to make fire, flint knapping was one of the first great technological advances in human prehistory. The simplest knapping technique is called "direct percussion". The piece of stone is struck with another rock or bit of wood to break smaller pieces off and gradually bring it into the desired shape.

This technique worked well when making simple clubs and hand axes, but it was not precise enough to make something as delicate as a knife blade. In order to avoid breaking the emerging tool itself during the knapping process, early humans developed a more controlled technique called "pressure flaking". The pressure flaker would refine the rough form of the stone by applying careful pressure with a pointed piece of antler. This process could be used to chip tiny fragments of stone away, gradually bringing the object into whatever precise shape was desired. A well-made

pressure-flaked knife is a thing of real beauty. The flaking scars are sometimes arranged with impressive forethought in flowing rows. In other cases the main body of the blade is ground and polished smooth, while the edges retain a contrasting fluted and serrated finish.

Stones suitable for knapping are found in a variety of colours in Europe and the Middle East, and it is clear that many of these appealed to Stone Age toolmakers. Flint occurs in many tints, ranging from a very light yellow through rich amber to dark brown and black. Quartzite appears in black tints, as well as in red, green and white.

RIGHT Striking the piece of flint would quickly break it. Instead, careful pressure is applied to remove one tiny fragment at a time.

The "Dagger Period" 1800–1500BC

Archaeological finds in Scandinavia have given us a good impression of how the best stone knives and daggers developed. The earliest examples from the Dagger Period have long, narrow blades and are roughly diamond-shaped in profile. One half of the diamond functioned as the grip or handle but was not as finely worked as the other end, the blade, which had precise pressure-flaked edges and a passable point.

ABOVE This detail of a giant statue of a pharaoh, *c.*1260BC, at the Amun Temple in Luxor, Egypt, shows a decorated dagger thrust into a belt. The grip is formed by two sculpted heads depicting the sun-god Ra.

The handle end on later examples gradually loses its taper, becoming more straight-sided, while the cross-section is rounder for a more comfortable grip. Finally, the butt of the handle becomes flared to improve the grip even further. The fully-fledged dagger of this period, in addition to the well-formed grip and butt, generally displays a graceful, leaf-shaped blade that has been cunningly strengthened by broadening and thickening only where necessary.

Flint knives in ancient Egypt

The ancient Egyptians also continued to make flint knives well into the Bronze Age. They served as the Egyptian warrior's sidearms long before any form of sword was known, and they continued to be used into the New Kingdom Period (*c.*1567–*c.*1085BC), by which time metal daggers were well known.

The earliest Egyptian flint knives date from the Early Dynastic Period (*c.*3100–*c.*2780BC). These weapons are easily recognizable by their broad, curved blades. On some examples the flaking pattern has been left over the whole surface of the blade, while others have been polished smooth. Grips were made of wood, horn or bone, and glued firmly in place. On rich examples this handle was sometimes covered with gold foil or carved with battle scenes. Shorter versions, at less than 30cm (12in) in length, were probably serviceable as fighting weapons, but the longer ones, 38cm (15in) or even longer, would have been quite fragile and may only have been used for ritual purposes.

ABOVE Found in Hindsgarl, Denmark, these flint daggers (*c.*1700BC) are typical of "Dagger Period" flint-work. The grips have imitation stitching to mimic the leather-bound handles of metal daggers of this period.

Most of the Later Dynastic (*c.*715–*c.*332 BC) and New Kingdom daggers were short, double-edged stabbing weapons, with simple hilts (handles), made of some organic material. New Kingdom daggers tend to be longer and narrower than older forms. Sometimes the grips also have a central rib or swelling.

Flint knives of pre-conquest America

The indigenous cultures of the Americas lived almost universally without metal tools and weapons until the first continuous contacts with Europeans in the 15th and 16th centuries AD. Before then, even in areas where the working of certain metals, primarily gold, was very advanced, tools and weapons remained entirely non-metallic. The ancient tribes inhabiting the present-day West Indies took advantage of the extremely hard woods found in the tropical lowlands to fashion clubs, swords and daggers, while obsidian was a common material used by the Aztecs of Mexico to fashion knives and daggers as well as the blades of their fierce-looking *macuauhuitl* sword-clubs. One chronicler of the Spanish Conquest of Mexico (1519–21) wrote that a native flint knife could cut "like a Toledo knife" – a reference to blades from the Spanish city, renowned for their high quality.

The end of the Stone Age

Stone was the best weapons material to which prehistoric humans had access. It was hard and dense, which meant that it could be given an extremely sharp edge. Even today, obsidian blades are used by optic surgeons because they are much sharper than any steel scalpels. But it was a very difficult material to work with and could only be made to assume a very restricted group of shapes. A stone blade, once broken, could never be repaired or recycled. These limitations led weapon makers to adopt a new material – metal.

ABOVE This striking flint knife blade is one of a number inlaid with stone of a contrasting colour. Found at Tenochtitlan in Mexico, the Aztec capital city, it dates from the Postclassic Period (*c.*AD1325–1521).

BELOW Ritual Egyptian knives of this type were the largest flint weapons ever made. This particular example, now missing its handle, dates from around 3000BC.

Copper, bronze and iron

The discovery of metalworking immeasurably improved the ability of early humans to construct edged weapons. Metal was flexible, much less brittle and more versatile than stone. It could be melted and cast into a huge variety of forms. When broken, it was possible to melt a metal weapon down and reform it. By the Bronze Age (*c*.3500–*c*.700BC), people were constructing more practical metallic fighting knives and daggers.

The first metal to be used for tools and weapons was copper. Small deposits of pure copper, which required no smelting (ore extraction) before working, were found in Mesopotamia, India, Egypt and North America. Copper weapons were being made in the Middle East as early as 6500BC, and in India by perhaps 6000BC. Pure copper weapons may have first been produced in North America by 5500BC, although the best evidence indicates a more recent date.

Between around 3000BC and 500BC, the "Old Copper Complex" people of the Great Lakes region of North America (Michigan and Wisconsin in the United States, and Ontario in Canada) were taking advantage of the pure copper nuggets found in that area to make knives and spearheads. These activities, along with later instances of copper working among native peoples along the northwest coast, remained the only examples of entirely indigenous metalwork practised by North American Indians until the arrival of Europeans in the 15th century AD.

The discovery of smelting

Naturally occurring pure metals were very scarce elsewhere and it was the invention of smelting that advanced the development of metalworking. The vast majority of the Earth's metals are contained within rock in the form of ore. Smelting is the process by which careful heating produces a chemical reaction that separates the metal from the surrounding materials. Once early humans had mastered this

ABOVE This 19th-century illustration is copied from an ancient Egyptian bas-relief depicting a metalworker forging a spear. The knowledge of smelting led the Egyptians and other ancient peoples to discover bronze.

process, their access to metals increased beyond measure. As a result, the rapid evolution of metal-edged weapons began.

Weapons made from copper

Copper is a resilient but very soft metal. Those who made copper weapons had to develop blade shapes that were structurally suited to the material, otherwise

BELOW Certain American Indian tribes have produced copper weapons for thousands of years. This 19th-century dagger, made by the Tlingit of southeastern Alaska and western Canada, has a copper blade.

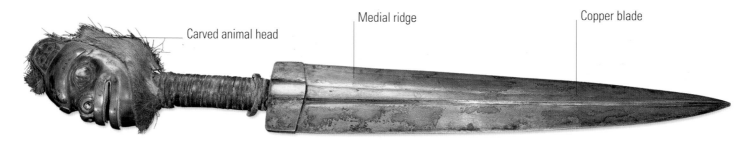

Carved animal head —   Medial ridge   Copper blade

Heavy pommel | Ridged grip | Medial ridge

a weapon would simply bend, crumple or collapse when it struck a blow. Daggers were undoubtedly the earliest metal-edged weapons made for fighting, simply because the softness of the material meant that a copper weapon had to be short and very broad. It was also necessary for a copper blade to be quite thick to give it some degree of stiffness. However, an increase in thickness produced an exponential (rather than proportionate) increase in weight, therefore a longer weapon such as a sword was out of the question. The earliest copper daggers had short, stout blades with a triangular outline that to some extent compensated for the softness of the metal. They were either cast in a mould or cut out and hammered into shape.

Early copper daggers were generally composed of a blade and a separate hilt of some hard organic material. Many excavated Mesopotamian graves of the Early Dynastic Period (*c.*2900–2330BC) have been found to include copper daggers of this type. Hilts were usually riveted to the wide base of the blade, although some surviving examples show no signs of rivets and so were presumably glued in place. A better

BELOW The usual form of bronze daggers was short and wide at the hilt to ensure strength. This example, dating from 2300–1800BC and found in Neuheiligen in Germany, also retains its metal hilt.

ABOVE The form of the latest metal weapons was copied in other materials. This Persian dagger of 1300–1200BC is not bronze but carved wood. The thick medial ridge or spine is designed to stiffen the blade.

BELOW The copper blade of this well-used Bronze Age knife, found in the River Thames in London, has been sharpened many times, grinding it down until only a small stub remains. The grip is a reconstruction.

answer appeared in the form of the tang; the base of the blade was drawn out again into a short, narrow rod, which could then be inserted into the hilt section.

Another key development in the design of early edged weapons was the medial ridge, or rib, cast into both sides of a blade using a two-piece mould. With a thick central spine, the rest of a blade could be made thinner and lighter. Its length and width could be increased, producing a more effective stabbing weapon. Daggers with these stiff medial ridges proliferated throughout the Middle East. The medial ridge was a pivotal development in the evolution of blade forms and remained an essential design element from the Bronze Age to the present day.

Cylindrical grip

Densely ridged blade

The introduction of bronze

Just as copper blades represented a great leap forward from the flint implements of prehistoric times, so too the discovery of bronze drove pure copper weapons into obsolescence. Bronze is an alloy, a mixture of two metals – copper and tin. A recipe for a good weapon was around nine parts bronze and one part tin, although exact proportions were at first hard to achieve. Bronze is harder than copper, resulting in stronger weapons that could take and hold a sharp edge better. Bronze blades could be made narrower and longer than copper ones.

Bronze flowed better than copper into moulds, which increased the possibilities for more elaborate and intricate designs. Hilts began to be cast in one piece with the blade, eliminating the weak point of a riveted joint between hilt and blade. Some of the earliest bronze daggers were

RIGHT This beautiful dagger hilt, made in Mycenae in around 1600BC, is decorated with inlaid lapis lazuli, crystal and gold. Two dragon heads form the guard.

ABOVE An exceptional number of Early Bronze Age weapons have been found at the site of the ancient Persian city of Luristan. This group includes wide-bladed cutting knives and narrow stabbing daggers.

made around 2500BC in the Sumerian city of Ur in Mesopotamia. These weapons have strong, ribbed blades and thick tangs. Early Bronze Age (*c*.3200–*c*.2800BC) daggers from Luristan (or Lorestan), an area in the west of modern Iran, were cast in one piece with recesses in the grip to take plates of wood or bone, the earliest known examples of grip "scales". These would later become some of the most common methods of grip construction in knife and dagger making throughout the world.

Mycenaean bronze daggers

Knowledge of bronze and bronze working moved gradually west from the Middle East through the Mediterranean and north into Europe, and by around 1600BC most of the peoples populating central and northern Europe were familiar

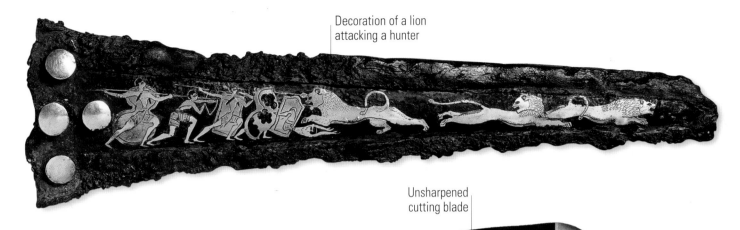

Decoration of a lion attacking a hunter

Unsharpened cutting blade

Sharpened stabbing blade

ABOVE A number of the surviving Mycenaean dagger blades carry superb inlaid decoration in gold, silver and niello (a black metal alloy). This blade features a lively hunting scene.

RIGHT After many sharpenings, what was once a wide-bladed, cutting knife could be transformed into a stout bronze needle, its sharpness making it an excellent stabbing weapon.

with it. In Greece, the bronze daggers of Mycenae (*c.*1600–1100BC) are particularly notable, not only because of the skill involved in their basic construction – the fine tapering blades once bearing handles of horn or ivory held in place with gold-capped rivets – but also for their exquisite decoration in gold and silver. Some exhibit well-studied depictions of marine life, while others bear hunting or battle scenes. These themes appealed to the warlike, seafaring Mycenaeans, who dominated the Aegean world by force from around 1400BC, during and after the collapse of the Minoan civilization (*c.*3400–*c.*1100BC). They also may have destroyed the city of Troy around 1180BC, thus forming the basis for the later Greek myth.

The knife becomes the dagger

By 1600BC, characteristic northern European bronze daggers were beginning to appear. One early form, typical of finds dating from around 1500–1450BC in the Rhône Valley, Gaul (present-day France), consisted of a short triangular blade with a rounded base onto which was riveted a hilt with a semicircular guard (protective plate), cylindrical grip and flat, circular butt (end). Metal hilts of this form, cast in one piece, quickly spread throughout France and across to Italy and other parts of central Europe.

Before the Middle Bronze Age (*c.*2800–*c.*1100BC) there is little point in discussing the differences between a dagger and any other sort of knife. But as people gained mastery over bronze, which allowed them to

diversify the styles and specific uses of weapons, clear differences began to appear. Simple bronze knives typical of the Middle Bronze Age in western Europe (*c.*1500–*c.*1100BC) have a wide cutting blade and usually a rounded tip – an all-purpose tool. But the cutting edges of a bronze blade had to be continually sharpened. Although it was harder than copper, bronze still could only hold an edge for a short period before use dulled it again. Constant sharpening, during which the edges were ground down using a whetstone, gradually narrowed the width of a knife, and after many sharpenings its size was much reduced and its shape dramatically altered; it became little more than a sharply tapered spike.

A knife's usefulness as a cutting tool over time was thus negligible, but undoubtedly humans soon discovered that such a tool could still be very effective when used exclusively as a stabbing weapon. It was not long before new weapons were being purposefully cast in this acutely pointed shape. During this period in history, dagger and knife became distinct from each other. The dagger was being used purely as a killing tool, almost exclusively for stabbing overarm or thrusting underarm, while a fighting knife remained more general in its applications. Of course, distinctions of this kind gloss over the huge grey areas that always exist between types, and so the present differentiation is meant only as a guiding generalization.

Medial ridge

Upward-curving pommel
arms or "antennae"

The Hallstatt culture (*c.*1200–500BC)

Hallstatt is a small lakeside town in Austria, southeast of Salzburg. In 1846 an enormous ancient cemetery was discovered there, and excavations carried out during the second half of the 19th century uncovered over 1,000 individual graves. The character of the material possessions found in the graves was very distinctive, being the earliest appearance of what is today often termed the "Celtic" style – organic, flowing forms that expressed the culture's close affinity with, and religious devotion to, the natural world. Objects of this style have since been found throughout Europe, and are collectively referred to as being part of the Hallstatt culture.

ABOVE This is a typical Hallstatt dagger, which is made of iron and dates from around 750–450BC. The dagger's blade is well formed for both cutting and thrusting actions.

The Hallstatt culture dominated most of Europe, in the east over most of what is now Austria, the Czech Republic, Slovakia, Slovenia, Croatia, Romania and Hungary, and in the west across Switzerland and parts of Italy, France and Germany. Its influence also extended to Spain and the British Isles. The culture is especially important because it forms a bridge between the Late Bronze Age (*c.*1100–800BC) and the earliest use of iron in Europe from around 800BC.

The dagger as a work of art

Until around 800BC, Hallstatt dagger blades were made of bronze, and indeed, bronze weapons continued to be used long after iron was well known throughout Europe. Hallstatt daggers are often exquisite works of art as well as weapons, having long, double-edged and multi-ridged blades. The hilts, usually made of bronze but sometimes covered in gold, were more intricate in their design than anything seen previously. The grips, rather than being just a simple cylinder, were gracefully tapered above and below a central swelling, in anticipation of the later Spanish and Roman versions of this design. Pommels (weights at the end of the hilt) took distinct forms. Some were of a flattened oval shape, usually fully pierced with designs. Others bore two intricate wheel-like structures on either side of a central block. Perhaps the most famous Hallstatt hilt was the so-called "antennae" type, the pommel being constructed of two upward-curving arms. Hallstatt daggers were also remarkable in that they were among the first European edged weapons to be made of a new material introduced from Asia – iron.

LEFT These two dagger hilts from northern Austria are excellent examples of the best Hallstatt craftsmanship. Their upward-curving pommel arms are distinguished by complex decorative forms.

Pommel wheel

Iron blade

Spherical chape

Scabbard

The coming of iron

Grave finds show that the Hallstatt peoples also had contact with Asia Minor – the origin of the earliest discovered iron weapons – from around 1000BC. It is believed that the first iron smelting began in Anatolia, eastern Turkey, about 1500BC. Initially the Hittites, who ruled this region (c.1900–700BC), guarded their discovery because of the great technological advantage that it gave them, but they could not restrict its proliferation for very long. Conquest and seafaring traders brought iron to the Biblical Middle East around 1000BC – the Bible mentions that Goliath carried a dagger of iron into battle – and trade across the Mediterranean brought iron to Greece and Italy by 700BC. The Hallstatt culture, being closely linked to these areas as well as directly to Asia Minor, therefore had multiple sources of iron at its disposal, and it is not at all surprising that the culture's later phases quickly brought the general use of iron to Europe.

The La Tène culture (*c.*500–0BC)

By around 400BC a different Celtic culture was taking over most of the areas previously dominated by the Hallstatt culture. Named after the area of the eastern end of Lake Neuchâtel in Switzerland where the first group of its objects were found, the La Tène culture represents the bulk of what modern people regard as Celtic. The weapons of this group of peoples usually display fantastic imagination and technical skill, their designs growing out of observations of the natural world that have been elaborated into a realm of wild abstraction, full of curving, twisting forms.

Most La Tène knives and daggers have blades of iron or steel, although the hilts were still often constructed of bronze. The double-edged daggers of the Hallstatt culture gave way to an increasing preference for broad, single-edged knives. A few double-edged daggers from the La Tène culture are known, and often these exhibit a development of the Hallstatt "antennae" hilt in which the horns of the pommel and guard have been made thicker and given spherical terminals; combined with an added spherical form at the base of the grip between the arms of the pommel, this gives the hilt a distinct anthropomorphic appearance: a small human figure in a spread-eagle position. The figure's head is also sometimes given realistic facial features.

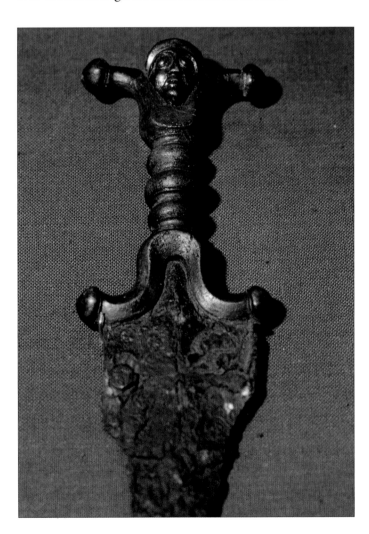

RIGHT This is an excellent example of the classic La Tène hilt of anthropomorphic form, depicting a stylized human figure. Hilts of this type are found on both daggers and swords.

Daggers of the Iron Age

The use of the dagger was not as common in the Iron Age (*c.*1400–*c.*500BC) as it had been throughout the preceding Bronze Age. Unlike their Minoan and Mycenaean ancestors, the warriors of Classical Greece (510–323BC) appear never to have employed the dagger as a military weapon, relying instead on the spear and sword. But in Italy, three vibrant cultures, the Villanovans, the Etruscans and the Romans, each developed forms of the dagger.

Bronze continued to be employed in the making of arms and armour throughout much of the Iron Age. Good-quality bronze was a harder metal than the earliest forms of iron, and it remained the preferred weapons material for a very long time. Iron was more easily sourced and therefore cheaper than the copper used to make bronze, and it had the potential to be forged into sharper- and harder-edged weapons. But the first iron-smelting processes were difficult and not very successful.

Early iron smelting

Metalworkers in the ancient world generally extracted copper metal from ore in furnaces designed to reach temperatures of between 700 and 900 degrees Celsius. It might have been possible to achieve the chemical reactions required to reduce iron from ore at 700 or 800 degrees, but the metal produced remained full of a glass-like substance called slag. This had to be liquefied to separate it from the iron, but this part of the process required a temperature of 1,200 degrees and so was beyond the technology of the time. Iron with a high slag content was brittle and inflexible, and therefore inferior to bronze. Only after metalworkers developed more advanced smelting processes, which could reach the higher temperatures, did they render bronze obsolete and turn to iron as the main raw material used to create weapons.

ABOVE A series of bronze Etruscan daggers found at Castione Marchesi in Italy. All display the typical steeply tapered blades, semi-circular guards and cylindrical grips that were common to this culture.

The Villanovans (*c.*1100–*c.*700BC) and Etruscans (*c.*800–*c.*100BC)

These technological difficulties meant that most daggers continued to be made of bronze, even after iron had been introduced. In Italy, the pre-Roman Villanovan and Etruscan cultures both favoured bronze as the material for edged weapons, even though they were both well aware of iron. The Villanovans were the first people on the Italian peninsula to work iron, and from them the technology passed to the Etruscans, who were dominant by the 8th century BC, passing from them to their enemies, the early Romans. However it was only with the rise of Rome as the supreme military power that iron came into widespread use.

RIGHT An Etruscan image of the war-god Mars. The Etruscans probably invested symbolic significance in their weapons – this dagger stands for masculinity and military might.

Wheel chape

Triple-button pommel

ABOVE This beautiful Villanovan dagger and scabbard, dating from the 6th–3rd century BC, is a good example of how the use of bronze continued well into the Iron Age.

Villanovan and Etruscan daggers are known in three main forms. Most have leaf-shaped blades although some have straight blades that taper sharply in the last third of their length and end in a thickened stabbing point. Others are triangular, with a consistent degree of taper from hilt to point. All three types include multiple ribs down their length.

The blade usually extended into a tang section at its base, onto which fitted a grip of stone, wood or bone. Some grips had "antennae pommels", which are a sign of Celtic influence, while others had simple T-shaped or disk pommels.

By the late 7th century BC the Etruscans had developed into the strongest military power on the Italian peninsula. They moved south over the River Tiber, taking many towns including Rome. The Etruscans retained their hold on southern Italy until 509BC, when the Romans rebelled and declared themselves a republic.

The Romans (800BC–AD410)

For over 1,000 years Rome maintained the fiercest, most disciplined and well-organized war machine in history. It adapted quickly to changes in enemy equipment and tactics, and often embraced them. Foreign innovations that were appropriated by the Romans included mail armour, armoured cavalry, the legendary *gladius*, or short sword, and the *pugio*, or dagger.

RIGHT Most of the earliest evidence for the pugio daggers adopted by the Romans comes from the Iberian Peninsula. This Iberian relief, from the 3rd century BC, shows a man armed with a dagger of pugio form.

FAR RIGHT This classic leaf-bladed Roman pugio blade with raised midrib dates from the 1st century AD. It is a well-designed weapon suitable for both slashing and thrusting attacks.

The Roman dagger appears to have been of Spanish origin. Examples from Numantia (in north-central Spain) dating from the 4th and 3rd centuries BC are virtually identical to daggers in the later years of the Roman Republic (509–27BC). However, it seems that the dagger was not immediately adopted by the Roman Army. It is not mentioned at all by Polybius (*c.*200–*c.*118BC), the Greek historian who described with great attention to detail the army of the Roman Republic. Initially the Romans seem to have thought of the dagger as a sort of trophy – an item of prestige that lent a certain military muscularity to a man's appearance. Perhaps a dagger pointed him out as someone who had fought for the Roman Republic in the wars abroad.

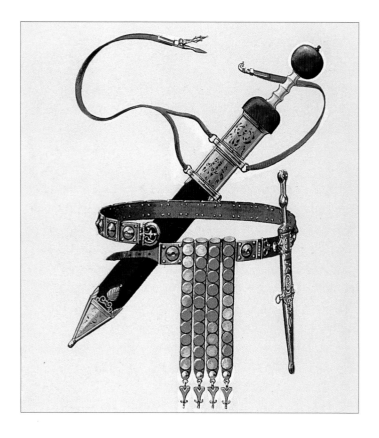

ABOVE The pugio was used in battle, for self-defence and also in the gladiatorial arena. This mosiac of around AD320 shows a gladiator pinning another to the ground while preparing to kill him with the dagger.

LEFT By the 1st century AD the pugio was part of a legionary's basic equipment, worn on the left of a belt that also held the plated *cingulum*.

The legionary pugio

The dagger became a standard part of Roman legionary equipment around the time of Christ. It was taken up as a complement to the sword, worn on the left side of the belt from which also hung the *cingulum*, or girdle. The sword was worn on the right side, suspended from a separate belt. Roman soldiers are frequently depicted armed in this way on tombstones and memorials, as well as in other forms of sculpture.

The pugio had a reasonably wide, waisted blade between 15–35cm (5.9–13.7in) in length. The point was frequently elongated to optimize its use for stabbing, while a strong midrib running down the length of the blade gave it additional strength and rigidity. The hand was protected by a simple guard riveted through the base of the blade, the arms of which sometimes extended a short distance beyond the edges of the blade, although many examples simply sit flush with the base. The pugio handle is very distinctive, having a circular swelling at its mid-point. Early pommels tend to be round, while later types usually have a flattened base or are even crescent-shaped. Generally, the pugio hilt was made in two halves – sometimes in bone or ivory but usually in bronze or iron – that sandwiched either side of the tang and were held in place by rivets through the guard, grip swelling and pommel. Although most pugio hilts were plain, high-status pieces were sometimes inlaid with precious metals.

The decline of the pugio

The legionary pugio dagger seems to have disappeared from use by Roman legionaries around AD200 or possibly earlier. Trajan's Column in Rome – completed AD113 to commemorate the Dacian campaigns of AD101–2 and AD104–6 – one of our most important sources for the appearance of Roman legionaries in the early 2nd century AD, does not include even one dagger. For whatever reason, the legionary pugio was discarded. A cruder form of this dagger continued to be used by auxiliary troops, soldiers from the Roman Empire's various outer territories. One spectacular find at Künzing, Bavaria, of the stock of a military workshop buried in the 3rd century AD, included 59 dagger blades and 29 sheaths. This indicates that the legionary pugio continued to be used as a military weapon long after it had been abandoned by the legions.

LEFT This Roman pugio, from southern Europe and made in the 1st century AD, retains its iron grip scales decorated with incised grooves and riveted to the blade tang.

The assassination of Julius Caesar, 44BC

In 44BC, Gaius Julius Caesar was the most powerful man in Rome. A great general, he had just been appointed dictator, although Rome was not yet an empire. The granting of absolute power to Julius Caesar was a key step in Rome's transition from a republican to an imperial state. Some members of the Roman senate opposed the slide into dictatorship, and a plot formed to assassinate Caesar.

On 15 March 44BC, Caesar went to a meeting at the request of the Senate to read a petition they wished to put to him. But the petition was a trick, conceived by the assassins, who called themselves "Liberators", to draw him into their trap. As he read the document one of the assassins drew his dagger and struck at Caesar's neck, but managed only to wound him slightly. The rest of the group (some accounts say up to 60 assailants) then attacked, stabbing their victim over and over, in the face, chest, shoulders and sides. Caesar tried to escape, but he stumbled and went down. The attackers continued their frenzied assault, which became so frantic that they accidentally stabbed each other as well as their victim. Caesar eventually died, his body covered in up to 35 stab wounds.

Roman coins commemorating the murder show the head of Brutus on one face and the assassins' daggers on the other: the pugio soon became the Roman legionary's constant companion.

LEFT Caesar's murder was commemorated on Roman coins of *c.*42BC that feature the profile head of Marcus Junius Brutus, leader of the conspiracy, on one side and pugios on the reverse.

BELOW The assassination in the Senate is here recreated by the German historical artist Heinrich Füger (1751-1818).

The Saxon fighting knife

The disintegration of the Roman Empire in the 5th century AD did not at first result in changes in weapons design and manufacture. The Empire's fragments initially tried to retain the trappings of imperial power, but it could not last. The old military structures gave way to much more variegated, clannish warrior cultures founded on personal loyalty and individual prowess. This social change was reflected in the design of weapons.

The collapse of Roman dominion in Europe led to many peoples between the 4th and 8th centuries AD (often called the "Migration Period") relocating in search of new prosperity and more fertile lands. Germanic tribes moved north from central Europe, while Scandinavian peoples struck west into Britain, Iceland, Greenland and North America.

The sax

Many Germanic tribes took advantage of the Romans' departure from Britain. While raids into Britain had begun before Roman withdrawal in AD410, they

ABOVE Found in the River Thames, this fine sax blade bears a unique inscription of the complete Anglo-Saxon runic alphabet and also the name of its maker or owner, Beagnoth.

increased dramatically afterwards. These invaders were generically referred to as "Saxons" even though their origins were diverse. Some seized parts of eastern Britain by force, while others allied themselves with the resident Romano-British peoples. Saxon warriors prized the sword above all weapons, but they also became known for a very distinctive fighting knife – the scramasax, seax or sax.

It has long been thought that the term "Saxon" expressed a characteristic preference for the "sax" as a weapon. Its use was not, however, limited to Britain. The earliest known Scandinavian sax dates from about 300BC, and its shape is much the same as those found in a bog at Vimose, on the Danish island of Funen, over six centuries later. In the Early Medieval Period (*c.*AD500–*c.*AD1100) the sax was the commonest sidearm of Saxons, Franks and Vikings, later examples having been found in Norway, Sweden, Denmark and mainland Europe.

Types of sax and their uses

The sax was a broad-bladed, single-edged fighting knife, the blade having a strong back and a wedge-shaped cross-section. Its length varied enormously. Smaller examples, almost "pen-knife" types, have blades as short as 7.5cm (3in) long, while the biggest sword versions are

LEFT Among the weapons found in France in a Merovingian grave of the third quarter of the 5th century AD was this early example of a sax, made of iron and with a finely decorated hilt.

Decorated blade

Wooden handle (now lost)

upwards of 76cm (30in) long. This very large form was called a langseax by the Viking spearmen who favoured it, while the average size, usually with a blade around 15cm (6in) long, was called a handseax. The blade was tapered sharply down its last third, and on the back only the cutting edge remained straight or slightly curved. There was no hand guard and only a simple grip of wood or bone. Sax blades could be very ornate, inlaid with copper, bronze and silver. Sometimes the name of the owner or maker was also inlaid, highlighting how important the sax was both as a prized weapon and as a signed work of art.

Although the sax may look more like a utilitarian, all-purpose knife, it was mainly a weapon for close-quarters combat. While the sword is the weapon most celebrated in early medieval literature, the sax makes several notable appearances. *The Tale of Thorstein Rod-Stroke* describes two men dying from fatal stab wounds dealt with a sax, while one of the most dramatic battlefield episodes occurred at the Battle of Bravoll around AD700, a contest for the Swedish throne between old King Harald War-Tooth and his nephew Sigurd. With most of his royal guard and champions dead or dying, King Harald charged his enemies with a sax in each hand, slaying many men before his skull was smashed by an axe-wielding foe.

Despite the sax's prominence in early medieval culture, the respect accorded fighting knives was minimal compared to the sword and spear. Even the Vikings could belittle the smaller forms of sax. In the Icelandic *Saga of Weapon's Fjord*, the warrior Geitir observes that "he with a little sax must try and try again".

ABOVE Found at Sittingbourne in England, this sax blade is ornately decorated with copper alloy and silver. One side carries the inscription "Sigebereht owns me", while the other reads "Biorhtelm made me".

Links between the sax and dagger

However popular the fighting knife was with individual warriors during the Migration Period and Early Middle Ages, its use was entirely a matter of personal preference. The dagger had not been a mandatory military requirement since it had ceased to be standard issue in the Roman Army. But the Franks under Charlemagne brought back many Roman ideas and regulations, including strict discipline and the use of armoured cavalry. In AD805, five years after being crowned with the title of "Emperor of the Romans", Charlemagne issued an edict that required all of his cavalry to be armed with a mail coat, sword, spear, shield and dagger.

Little is known about the transition from the later saxes of the 11th century to the "knightly" daggers of the 13th and 14th centuries. Many Anglo-Saxons at the Battle of Hastings in 1066 probably carried long saxes, while their Norman enemies, themselves descended from the Vikings, may have been armed with smaller sax-like knives in addition to their swords and spears. Indeed, the sax may not have fallen out of fashion at all; knives looking very much like the sax were still being made in England during the 1400s.

BELOW These two excavated sax blades give a good impression of the more typical proportions of these famous weapons. Found in central Europe, they probably date from the 6th–8th centuries AD.

Medieval daggers

The Medieval Period (*c.*1100–*c.*1450) was the age of the knight and of chivalry. The culture of the mounted warrior changed how combat was conducted and led to a reconsideration of how weapons were used. Knights initially thought the dagger to be unimportant, but by the 14th century it had become an essential part of their equipment. Dagger types evolved and multiplied. Their new significance applied on the battlefield as well as in civilian life.

The use of the dagger had remained a matter of personal preference since its requirement by the Roman legions had been dropped in the 2nd century AD. All manner of knives were no doubt carried by fighting men, but there were no specific regulations or accepted practice. The AD805 edict of the Holy Roman Emperor Charlemagne that all imperial cavalrymen should carry the dagger was significant, but several hundred years would pass before Charlemagne's lead was followed.

The unworthy dagger

During the 12th and 13th centuries, daggers do not seem to have been thought worthy of much notice. Since Roman times, the respected weapons of the elite warrior were the spear and the sword. Daggers rarely appear on the funerary monuments of knights of this period, nor do we find dagger combat depicted in art until around 1250. Perhaps because it was advocated only as a last resort when all other weapons were broken or lost, the dagger does not seem to have interested artists until the middle of the 13th century.

The dagger in the 12th century sometimes carried derogatory associations. Usually called a cultellus or coustel, it was commonly connected with criminals; *coustiller* and *cultellarius* were both terms used to refer to thieves, thugs and bandits. A statute of 1152 issued by the Count of Toulouse in France refers to "evil men, called coustillers, who cause havoc with their daggers after nightfall".

BELOW This detail from a 13th-century manuscript version of the Old Testament shows men armed in the style of the time. One of the central figures can be seen stabbing his enemy with a short dagger.

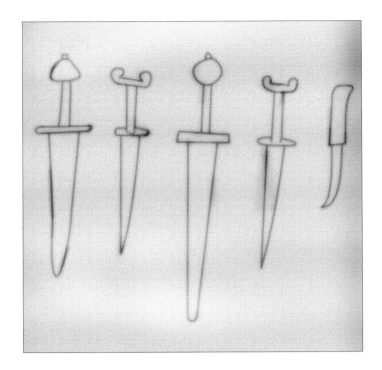

LEFT This illustration, after an 11th-century Italian manuscript, shows the medieval distinction between the two main dagger types: the wide-bladed cutting daggers and the narrow stabbing daggers.

Miséricorde

The word *miséricorde*, meaning mercy or pity, began to be used in the mid-13th century to refer to the dagger wielded by knights. It is commonly thought that the word association comes from the use of the dagger for the mercy killing of wounded men on the battlefield. In fact, it's more likely that it derives from the dagger's effectiveness in compelling an overthrown knight to surrender – with a request for mercy – to avoid being slain in single combat.

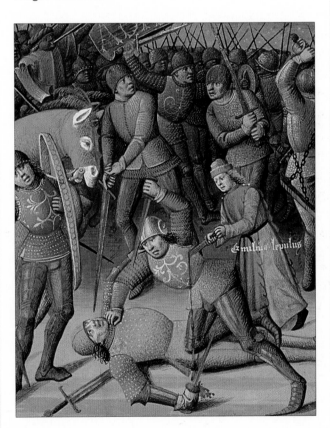

ABOVE This 15th-century manuscript detail shows an armoured warrior preparing to either accept his enemy's surrender or finish the fight with a deadly downward dagger blow.

Cutting daggers and stabbing daggers

Despite its wicked reputation, the dagger evolved quickly during the 13th and 14th centuries. By 1300 it was a standard part of the knight's armament, along with the lance, sword and axe or mace. Some daggers remained closely related to knives intended for general use. But others became removed from anything resembling an all-purpose blade, being instead dedicated exclusively to killing people.

Distinctions were clearly being made by the beginning of the 14th century. An inventory of the weapons belonging to Raoul de Nesle, Constable of France, taken after he was killed in 1302, employs specific terminology for two sorts of dagger. The broader-bladed daggers, those resembling utilitarian knives, are called coutiaus à tailler, or cutting daggers. These are distinguished from the coutiaus à pointe, or stabbing daggers.

A number of daggers from this period survive, and they clearly illustrate both types. The cutting daggers are frequently single-edged, with a strong back, the point tapering on the sharp side only, much like a kitchen knife. Stabbing daggers are much longer, narrower and very sharply tapered. By 1375, some forms of stabbing dagger could hardly be considered edged weapons at all; their blades, having no cutting edges, are little more than reinforced spikes of hardened steel for punching through muscle and bone. With enough force behind them, these blades, like giant awls, could probably also pierce the padded textile, mail and light plate armour of the time.

As blade forms multiplied, so did the forms of dagger hilt. Grouped according to the hilt form, there were four primary types of dagger in common use during the Medieval Period.

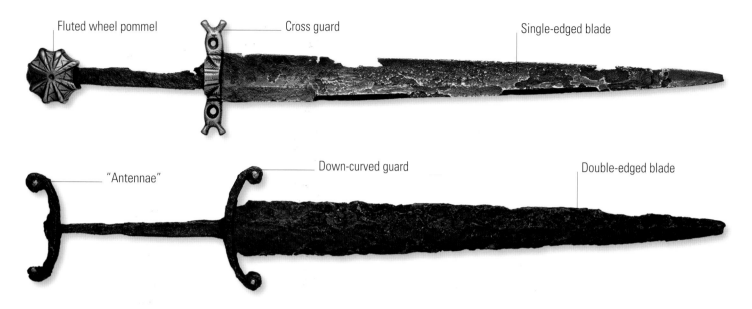

Fluted wheel pommel   Cross guard   Single-edged blade

"Antennae"   Down-curved guard   Double-edged blade

Cross-hilt daggers

The first daggers to be generally adopted in the 12th and 13th centuries had simple cross hilts, like diminutive swords. These are often called "quillon" daggers, although this is a post-medieval term (referring to the arms of the cross guard, the bar across the hilt).

Most early cross-hilt daggers have a short cross guard, drooping downwards towards the blade, and a crescent-shaped pommel. Some pommels are in fact more suggestive of a pair of horns, very like the Bronze Age "antennae" and "anthropomorphic" daggers of the Hallstatt and La Tène cultures described earlier.

While medieval cross-hilt daggers with "antennae" pommels seem to have gone out of fashion around 1350, versions with the crescent-shaped pommel continued to be popular into the 15th century; a related group of daggers also exhibit pommels wherein the crescent horns have been brought together to form a fully enclosed ring. Cross-hilt daggers also appear after 1350 with pommels shaped like stars, shields or mushrooms. Polygonal and wheel-type pommels were also common. Richer examples were sometimes decorated with the heraldic arms of the owner, in paint, enamel, gold and silver.

Cross-hilt daggers in art are shown being used both overarm, held with the blade projecting downwards from the base of the fist, and underarm with the blade projecting upwards. But as the 14th century progressed, the exclusive practice of overarm, blade-downwards fighting techniques dominated, and this was reflected in the development of dagger hilts. Some daggers are difficult to hold in any position other than blade-downwards. Well-made weapons often express how

TOP Although their cross guard construction was simple, many medieval daggers have sculpted pommels and guards. This 15th-century cross-hilt dagger has a pommel and guard of copper alloy cast into ornate forms.

ABOVE Certain medieval daggers such as this 14th-century English cross-hilt example bear some resemblance to the earlier Hallstatt types, having comparable "antennae" pommels.

they "wish" to be used when handled, and it is certainly the case that many medieval daggers feel natural and comfortable when held with the blade downwards, but become remarkably awkward when reversed.

The baselard

This dagger was developed in the late 13th century for civilian as well as military use. Especially popular in Italy, but also found in English art of the 14th century, the baselard may have originated in Switzerland, in the city of Basel. An English song dating from the early 15th century neatly expresses how widespread the baselard had become by that time:

There is no man worth a leak,
Be he sturdy, be he meek
But he bear a baselard.

The baselard is recognized by its distinctive hilt, which is again reminiscent of the Hallstatt culture. Baselard hilts are usually shaped like a capital "I" or an upended "H", the bottom cross piece often being wider than the one that forms the guard. The tang is cut to the shape of the whole hilt and sandwiched between plates usually of wood, and the whole assembly is then riveted together. Baselard blades could be either single-

The overarm blow

Humans and many of the great apes instinctively employ the overarm blow struck with the base of the fist. In humans this in-built attack pattern is commonly observed in young children who, when sufficiently annoyed, almost always employ what is sometimes called "the beating movement", striking their source of frustration with elbow bent and arm raised at the shoulder, the fist or open hand then being brought down with great force.

Overarm stabbing blows with a downward-pointing blade can be much more powerful than an underarm thrust. Medieval dagger fighting adopted this instinctive defensive movement and combined it with a weapon well suited to that mode of attack. When used correctly by an expert martial artist such as a knight, who learned his fighting skills as a child and perfected them over many years of constant practice, such a technique became horrifyingly effective. Fought at close range, dagger combat would almost without question lead to serious or fatal injury. As one 15th-century German fight master wrote in his manual on martial arts: "Now we come to the dagger; God help us all!"

ABOVE This French medieval illustration of a disagreement shows daggers drawn in *The Argument*, from a late 15th-century copy of *The Book of Good Morals* by Jacques le Grant.

Asymmetrical pommel

Finger grooves

Fire-gilt fuller

Medial ridge

Single cutting edge

ABOVE The I-shaped baselard hilt is seen clearly in these examples. The English type on the left has a long cut-and-thrust blade. The broad-bladed European dagger is an earlier design.

or double-edged, and were generally quite broad. They could also be quite long, more like short swords. The longer forms, however, were not as common as the shorter ones, tending to be more exclusively Swiss.

When worn by warriors, baselards were slung on the right hip, but in civilian life they were usually worn centrally below the waist. From this position the dagger could be swiftly drawn. This method of wearing the dagger could never have avoided the inevitable associations with the erect male genitalia, and from the fashion of wearing the dagger over the groin developed one of the most famous of all European dagger types.

"Trumpet" grip

Single-edged blade

Rondel guard

Tapered thrusting point

The ballock dagger

Medieval culture was full of phallic imagery and it was flaunted rather than hidden. The ballock dagger, which appeared around 1300, was the logical development of the fashion for centrally slung weapons. The hilt was carved out of a single piece of wood and shaped to resemble an erect penis and testicles, with a bulbous pommel and a rounded lobe on either side of the blade in place of the guard. Some examples are very lifelike while others are more stylized.

Despite the apparently unavoidable inspiration for this dagger's distinctive form, the selective

TOP This English ballock dagger, dating from the 15th century, is an early example of the slightly less phallic "trumpet" type, which remained common in the early 16th century.

ABOVE Earlier rondel daggers such as this 14th-century English weapon often have rondels that are reasonably thick; they are frequently made of wood sandwiched between metal disks.

interpretation of the Middle Ages propagated in the 19th century casts a long shadow. The Victorians prudishly renamed these weapons "kidney" daggers, a ridiculous denial of the obvious but one that has survived in usage until very recently.

An important variation of the classic ballock hilt appeared in the 15th century. Here, rather than being surmounted by a bulbous head, the grip flared out almost like a trumpet. The flat-top surface of this flared end was usually capped with a metal disk-shaped plate, often engraved with geometric or vegetal designs. This form never replaced the earlier type, but rather they coexisted well into the 16th century.

The form of blades attached to these hilts varied enormously. The most usual form is triangular in cross-section and tapers consistently from base to point. By the late 14th century, other versions had evolved with square-sectioned tips, to strengthen them for stabbing. Double-edged blades were also fitted to the hilts, although these could never be as wide at the base as those found on baselards, for example; the ballock hilt always required a comparatively narrow blade.

LEFT This detail from *The National Law Codes of Magnus Eriksson* (c.1450) shows the enactment of a violent crime. The distinctive hilt of a ballock dagger can be seen protruding from the victim's chest.

The rondel dagger

It is difficult to be sure when the fourth medieval form of dagger, the rondel dagger, first appeared but it was common by 1350; it may have been known since about 1300. The hilt comprised a grip situated between two disk-shaped "rondels". These gave good protection to the hand while also acting as stops to prevent the hand slipping when a downward stabbing blow was struck. Its use spread over an exceptionally large area, including all of western, central and northern Europe, and even stretching into Poland, and lasted until the mid-16th century.

At first only the guard of rondel-type daggers was disk-shaped, the pommel being polygonal or rounded. But the pommel was soon replaced by another rondel, and the true rondel dagger rapidly assumed an almost universal status as the favourite dagger of knights and men-at-arms. Usually the rondels were strictly circular, although some were faceted, fluted or cusped. The blades tended to be double-edged at first, of flattened diamond section, sometimes even having a central fuller (shallow weight-reducing groove).

After 1400 the rondel dagger evolved considerably. The rondels were made in a number of different ways. Sometimes they were made of wood faced with metal, although more often they were made solely of steel, iron or copper alloy. By the middle of the 15th century, some of the more ornate daggers had rondels built up of multiple disks of different materials – white and yellow metal, but also horn, wood and bone. When smoothed and polished, the edges of these rondels displayed very attractive, multicoloured strata. Sometimes the layering was enhanced with octagonal or hexagonal rather than circular layers.

Rondel dagger grips were constructed in both of the usual ways. Either the tang was made narrow so that it could pass down the centre of the length of the grip to be hammered over on top of the pommel, or it was kept wide and filed into the desired grip shape, with the grip made in two halves, then being riveted onto it on either side.

The basic shape was cylindrical, often widening slightly in the middle and tapering down at either end. Many grip shapes were never more ornate than this simple form. The grip could also be decorated. The more elaborate examples, in particular, tend to be carved or embellished in some way.

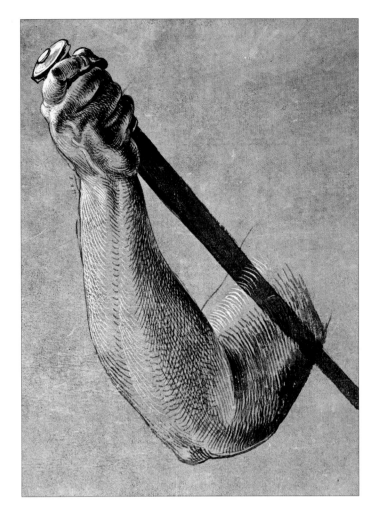

ABOVE This sketch by the German artist Albrecht Dürer is a study of a hand grasping a rondel dagger in the action of plunging it into the chest. It was made in preparation for his painting *The Suicide of Lucretia,* 1518.

Spiral carving was particularly fashionable. The finest examples were made entirely of metal, engraved with intricate designs. Only fragments of these more ornate, knightly rondel daggers survive, although they are depicted frequently on funerary effigies, complete with their exquisitely tooled scabbards. Such elaborate decorated weapons were obvious status symbols.

BELOW Some rondel daggers were extremely ornate. This fragment is all that remains of a once stunning English 15th-century weapon, probably that of a knight. The hilt was entirely fire-gilt (gilded with a heated mix of gold and mercury) and incised with geometric patterns.

Daggers of the Renaissance

Each of the medieval dagger types remained in use throughout the 16th and into the 17th century. Some remained largely unchanged, while others evolved according to more restricted regional fashions. Although in the 16th century the Renaissance dagger was still an important military weapon, it was becoming more common in everyday life and was just as likely to be drawn in a royal palace or urban back alley as on the battlefield.

The 1500s were the golden age of the dagger in Europe. During this century aristocratic fashions in clothes and behaviour became more decadent and extravagant. Nobles dripped with jewels and precious stones, their clothing intricately constructed using many different materials. Individuality had become

LEFT Renaissance daggers were often glamorous fashion accessories, as shown by this south German cross-hilt dagger with a curved blade and hilt with gold, gemstones and cameos.

much more important than it ever had been before, and rich people were anxious to express themselves as individuals through material display. With fine clothes went fine weapons, and the dagger was ever-present, not just as a tool and a weapon but now also as an indispensable fashion accessory.

The assassin's choice

The dagger had been a weapon favoured by assassins since ancient times because its small size made it easy to hide. If discovered its presence could be easily explained, since a knife was routinely carried by most people. During the Renaissance, assassination became more common, particularly in the ruthless political environment of the time. Many rulers and statesmen fell under plunging dagger blades.

One case, which occurred in 1537, was that of Alessandro de' Medici, Duke of Florence, who was lured away from his bodyguards by the temptation of a sexual encounter with the beautiful sister of Lorenzino de' Medici ("Bad Lorenzino"), a distant cousin. Once alone, Alessandro was ambushed and stabbed to death by Lorenzino, who later claimed that he had killed Alessandro for the sake of the Florentine Republic, comparing his deed to Brutus' murder of Julius Caesar. Lorenzino was himself stabbed to death in Venice a year later.

ABOVE The dagger was the constant companion of the Renaissance nobleman. Hans Holbein's 1534 portrait of Charles de Solier, the French envoy at the court of Henry VIII, shows the lord with a fine gilded dagger.

RIGHT A number of Renaissance rulers met a grisly end on the point of an assassin's dagger. In 1589 King Henry III of France was stabbed to death by a Dominican friar, who was then killed by the royal guard.

The landsknecht daggers

The modern term "landsknecht" dagger actually refers to three quite different forms, and is somewhat misleading in any case. The Landsknechts were predominantly German, Swiss and Flemish mercenaries who took part in almost every military campaign of the 16th century and were famous for their flamboyant "puffed and slashed" clothing.

Only the first type of so-called landsknecht dagger can be directly associated with these fierce professional soldiers. Both the two-handed great sword and smaller arming sword, or katzbalger, of the Landsknecht have a characteristic form of guard – the long arms are bent into a nearly circular S-shape. This first class of landsknecht dagger has a guard similarly formed, and its pommel also takes the same flaring form found on surviving katzbalgers. The blade is usually double-edged and tapered evenly from guard to point.

Unlike the first type, there is no stylistic similarity between the second type and the other characteristic landsknecht weapons familiar from pictorial representations. It may be an offshoot of the rondel dagger. One of its defining features is a grip that flares, trumpet-like, towards the pommel, the end of which is covered either with a flat metal disk or a domed plate. The guard is usually formed of a small plate cut into three lobes (rounded projections), which bend down towards the blade like drooping leaves. The length of the scabbard is divided by groups of two or three rings,

RIGHT A number of Renaissance rulers met a grisly end on the point of an assassin's dagger. In 1589 King Henry III of France was stabbed to death by a Dominican friar, who was then killed by the royal guard.

wider than the scabbard itself. On finer examples, some or all of the rings are repeatedly sawn vertically, giving the scabbard an appearance in keeping with the elaborate puffed and slashed clothing of the time.

The third type of dagger in this group is essentially a type of cross-hilt dagger. It is also one of the earliest forms to carry a side ring, placed centrally on the outside of the guard to give added protection to the knuckles. This type is also called a Saxon dagger, as many of them were made in eastern parts of the German Empire. The pommels of these Saxon daggers are usually pear-shaped or conical and often capped with a silver plate. Both this plate and the guard are frequently engraved with floral designs, and the grip is wrapped with fine twisted wire. Saxon dagger scabbards often have silver mounts engraved to match the pommel cap (decorative covering) and guard.

S-shaped *katzbalger* guard

Cast copper alloy handle

ABOVE This landsknecht dagger's distinctive hilt matches the short and two-handed swords favoured by these renowned mercenaries. Only a very few of these daggers survive today.

Short baluster-turned guard

Side ring

Decorated silver pommel cap

Double-edged blade

ABOVE This silver-decorated Saxon dagger is another common landsknecht type. It was made during the 16th century.

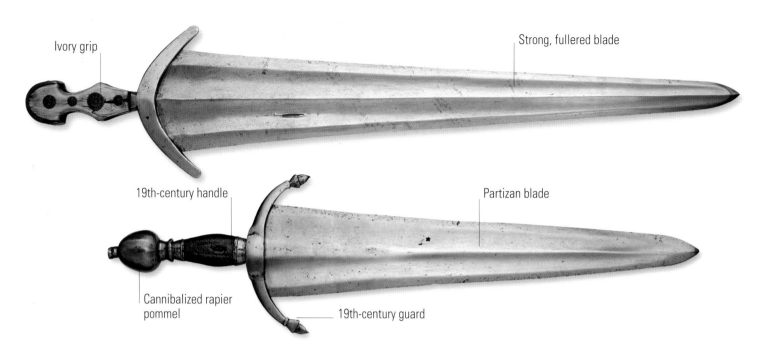

Ivory grip

Strong, fullered blade

19th-century handle

Partizan blade

Cannibalized rapier pommel

19th-century guard

TOP Small cinquedeas are easily classified as daggers, but many have blade lengths closer to short swords. They make effective concussive cut-and-thrust weapons, unlike practically all forms of dagger.

ABOVE Because of their close associations with the Renaissance, cinquedeas were often copied in the 19th century. This fake was built using a staff weapon blade and various other sword hilt parts.

The cinquedea

This type of large Italian dagger is often thought to have gained its name because its extreme width at the guard is about as wide as a man's hand. Since the Italian for "five fingers" is *cinque diti*, this is not an entirely unreasonable assumption. But it is probably not correct. An early 17th-century definition of a cinquedea refers to a Venetian dagger that was five fingers long, not five fingers wide, and the term itself appears not to have been in use earlier than the late 16th century, some time after the supposed cinquedea fell out of fashion. Despite the fact that the use of the term is probably not consistent with the weapon's original historical context, roughly 1450–1520, its present meaning is now universally understood.

The cinquedea was a weapon of high status. The double-edged blade, very wide at the guard, tapered steeply to the point, took the form of a long isosceles triangle and was forged with a series of ridges running down the length of the blade. Two parallel ridges were normally located near the point, these increasing to three in the middle of the blade, with a final set of four at

RIGHT The cinquedea may have been based on weapons of the ancient world such as this Bronze Age Etruscan dagger. Renaissance artists drew much inspiration from ancient Greek and Roman art.

the base. By 1500, cinquedea blades were being elaborately decorated with etched Neo-classical designs or scenes from ancient Greco-Roman myths, as well as with fire gilding and even heat blueing (the application of controlled heat).

The cinquedea hilt was just as distinctive as its blade. The guard was formed into a graceful arch, the arms curving downwards towards the blade, and was often drawn to a point in the centre. Because of the extreme width of the base of the blade, only the tips of the arms extended beyond its edges. The guard was also often etched with twisting vines or foliated scrolls. The ergonomic grip, usually plated with bone or ivory, was scooped out on either side to produce recesses for the fingers on both sides of a central swelling. The tubular rivets holding the ivory or bone plates to the tang were generally filled in with inserts beautifully pierced with geometric designs. The rounded pommel, made in one piece with the grip, was usually covered with a piece of gilded metal.

It is tempting to suggest that the cinquedea was just one of the many products of the infatuation with classical art and culture that characterized the Renaissance Period. The cinquedea certainly resembles some types of wide-bladed Bronze Age dagger. Perhaps the Italian dagger is a direct emulation by Renaissance smiths of an ancient design.

The ear dagger

Daggers of eared form may have appeared as early as the 14th century, but their greatest period of popularity occurred during the first half of the 16th century. The ear dagger probably originated in Spain, a result of the influence of Islamic design on the tastes of the Iberian nobility. Eared daggers were being made in Persia during the Bronze Age, and the design remained popular for both sword and dagger hilts throughout the Middle East, or "Levant" as the region was called by Renaissance Europeans. Indeed, the ear dagger was referred to in Italy as *alla Levantina*, a term that clearly demonstrates the perceived origin of the design.

The ears of the hilt are usually formed as extensions of the very thick tang, which have been hammered out to create the disk-shaped "ears" diverging at sharp angles from the bottom of the grip. The ears were generally faced with plates of ivory, horn or bone. The grip is generally quite narrow, with a slight central swelling. While the earliest ear daggers appear to have had guards not unlike those on rondel daggers, by the 16th century the guard had shrunk to little more than a small anvil or block-shaped spacer, which was plated with the same organic material as the grip and ears.

Ear-dagger blades are invariably double-edged, one edge often beginning lower on the ricasso (the flattened square of blade near the guard) than the other, producing an odd but pleasing offset effect. Some also have specially thickened stabbing points.

The ricasso, exposed sides of the tang and area between the ears are sometimes damascened (woven) in gold. One of the most famous makers of ear daggers was Diego de Çaias, a Spanish maker of high-quality weapons in the 1530s and 1540s who was patronized by Francis I of France and Henry VIII of England.

BELOW Ear daggers are like no other form of European dagger, displaying a distinct Middle Eastern inspiration. This early 16th-century example is Italian, although many others were made in Spain.

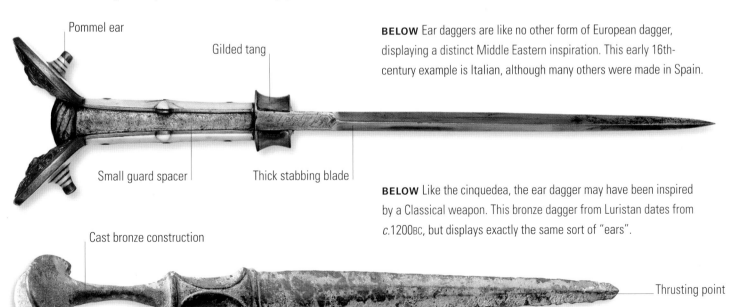

Pommel ear

Gilded tang

Small guard spacer

Thick stabbing blade

Cast bronze construction

BELOW Like the cinquedea, the ear dagger may have been inspired by a Classical weapon. This bronze dagger from Luristan dates from *c.*1200BC, but displays exactly the same sort of "ears".

Thrusting point

Metal pommel-plate

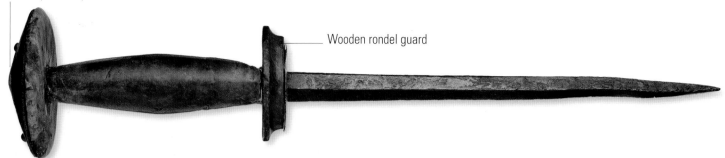

Wooden rondel guard

Medieval daggers of the 16th century

In addition to the ear dagger, other forms of dagger that had developed during the Middle Ages continued to be made throughout the 16th century. The most common types, prevalent throughout Europe, were cross-hilt daggers. Smaller versions continued to be

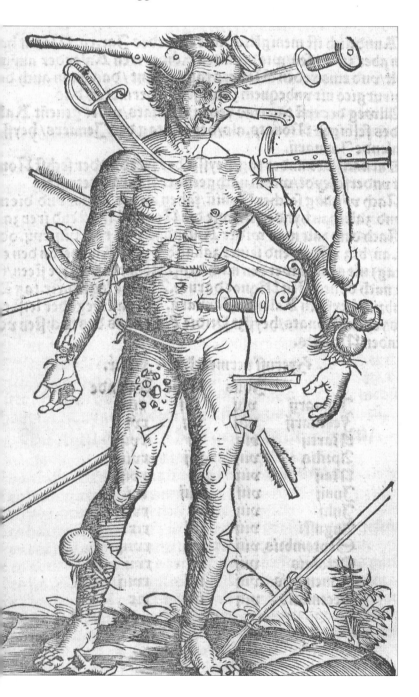

ABOVE Despite the fact that the production of rondel daggers seems to have declined quickly after 1500, older weapons such as this late-medieval example, would have remained in use for much longer.

carried for general last-ditch self-defence by both armoured warriors and by civilians, while larger forms had begun to be incorporated into the latest fencing styles by the middle of the century. Ballock daggers also continued to be made in both of their distinctive forms. The grips were still made primarily in wood, although ivory and even agate examples are known. Later ballock dagger blades tend to be very narrow and double-edged, although in some cases they are little more than four-sided spikes.

Rondel daggers, so ubiquitous during the 14th and 15th centuries, seem to have quickly fallen out of favour in the 16th century, either evolving into new forms such as certain of the landsknecht dagger types, or disappearing altogether.

"Swiss" and "Holbein" daggers

Another medieval dagger that developed into a new and distinct form was the baselard. The essential form of what became the 16th-century "Swiss" dagger appeared in the last 20 years or so of the 15th century, when the I-shaped hilt of the baselard developed inward-curving arms, strengthened with metal sleeves, at either end of the grip. The blade of the short-sword type of "Swiss" baselard was shortened to dagger length, but unusually retained its greater width and displayed a slight leaf shape. Apart from a single fuller, "Swiss" dagger blades were left entirely plain. Unlike the earlier baselard, on which the arms of the hilt were formed by the tang over which were laid plates of wood, the hilt of the 16th-century "Swiss" dagger was carved from a single

LEFT The "wound man" figure illustrated common injuries in Renaissance surgical texts. This German version from 1528 includes rondel dagger and knife stab wounds to the abdomen, face and head.

RIGHT In addition to the T-shaped hilt and ornate scabbard, the typical "Swiss" dagger also included a byknife and awl. Decorated to match the scabbard, these fitted into special sleeves in the outer side.

Byknives

Wooden grip

Foliate scabbard chape

Double-edged blade

piece of hardwood, the sides of the grip were faceted and the centre was drilled out for the insertion of the narrow tang.

"Swiss" daggers are perhaps most famous for their very elaborate scabbards. The earliest examples were made of wood covered in leather, with a simple metal locket (fitting at the mouth of the scabbard) and chape (fitting at the tip of the scabbard). But after 1510, the metal mounts developed rapidly until the whole front of the scabbard was covered in silver or gilt. This decorative metal sleeve was cast with elaborate, pierced designs in relief, which were often engraved as well to add an additional level of detail.

A number of famous Swiss artists created designs for the decoration of these dagger sleeves, including Urs Graf, Heinrich Aldegrever and Hans Holbein the Younger. These designs usually involved Biblical or mythological scenes. One of Holbein's designs, for which the original drawings survive, depicted the Dance of Death, a popular allegory that expressed the universal nature of death. Death is portrayed as a re-animated skeleton, which dances with people from all levels of society. This design became so common that these weapons are often called "Holbein" daggers.

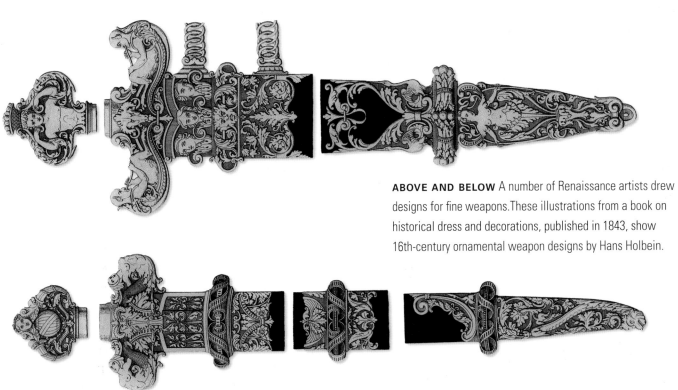

ABOVE AND BELOW A number of Renaissance artists drew designs for fine weapons. These illustrations from a book on historical dress and decorations, published in 1843, show 16th-century ornamental weapon designs by Hans Holbein.

Daggers for the Renaissance duel

The dagger forms had diversified in the 14th and 15th centuries, but the fighting methods that employed them had not changed very much by the 1500s – these same basic rondel, ballock and cross-hilted weapons continued to be drawn as a last resort on the battlefield and in daily life. But the new Renaissance fashion for civilian swordmanship also led to new more specialized daggers, intended to be used exclusively as "defencing" weapons.

Renaissance society was strongly influenced by the rise of a new non-noble class who, despite their lack of aristocratic status, were often wealthy and upwardly mobile. Now it was not just the nobility who could afford luxuries such as fine clothes and weapons. The middle class was just as likely as the aristocracy (if not more so) to want to follow the latest fashions and to have the means to do so. They quickly appropriated a number of the traditional status symbols that in the past had always been exclusive to the nobility.

ABOVE Once the art of fighting with the rapier and dagger had become fashionable, weapons makers began producing fine sets with matching decoration. This exceptional Italian set, made in *c.*1600, features sumptuous inlaid and relief ornament.

LEFT The expensively decorated rapier and dagger set was an integral part of a gentleman's rich attire, as can be seen in Nicolas Neufchatel's portrait of Hieronimus Koler (1528–1573).

The sword enters civilian life

One of the most important new symbols of social status adopted by the *nouveau riche* was the sword. In the Medieval Period the sword had been a knightly weapon; it was expensive and its use required many years of dedicated practice. More importantly, the use of the sword in dealing with personal grievances – through trial by combat – was a right restricted to the nobility. By the mid-16th century, most non-noble gentlemen had adopted the sword as a sign of their own economic "nobility". More importantly, they began to wear it at all times. This was a new development; before the 16th century the sword

was never worn with civilian dress except when travelling. This change in the acceptance of weapons in society was observed by the 16th-century chronicler Claude Haton, leading him to write, of the year 1555: "There is no mother's son at this time who did not carry a sword or a dagger."

The duel

These new civilian swords brought with them a perceived right to address personal grievances and disagreements through violence; with weapons close to hand they were more easily drawn in anger, and quickly became a first reaction rather than a last resort. But the autonomous right to settle personal disputes with violence was a right restricted to the aristocracy. This made it a luxury that the middle class wanted. The ancient practice of judicial combat was seized upon by fashionable society and twisted into the private duel, fought anywhere and at any time, often for the most trivial reasons.

Duelling quickly became a craze. Hundreds and then thousands of men were killed each year during the second half of the 16th century, all in supposed "affairs of honour". These disputes could be caused by a verbal slight, physical altercation or even an insulting glance. Sir Walter Raleigh – the famous Elizabethan explorer who established one of the earliest American colonies at Roanoke Island in what is today North Carolina – wrote earnestly that "to give the lie deserves no less than stabbin". It was this brutal subculture that led to a number of key innovations in the design and use of edged weapons.

ABOVE The weapons in legal judicial duels were often the sword and shield, as in this trial by combat fought in Paris in 1547. For impromptu, illegal combats the inconvenient shield was supplanted by the dagger.

BELOW Sometimes there is more to a rapier and dagger set than meets the eye. This unique set, by Tobias Reichel of Dresden, *c.*1610, includes tiny timepieces hidden in the pommels.

Combat with rapier and dagger

Once the sword was introduced into this new civilian fighting environment, it began to change. Plate armour was not worn in daily life, and so swords began to be designed especially to take on vulnerable but quicker opponents. The use of the thrust became much more important, and sword blades became longer and longer, as the control of distance and the ability to kill an enemy without getting too close became central to civilian fighting styles. By the second half of the 16th century, the civilian sword had evolved into something entirely unlike its military counterpart. The blade was much longer, narrower and thickened down its spine so that it was as ridged as possible, and the hilt – which now had to protect the unarmoured hand – had a number of additional sweeping bars and ring guards added to it. This non-military sword was called *espada ropera* in Spanish, "sword of the robe", or a sword to be worn with civilian clothing. The French called it *épée rapière*, which in turn became the English "rapier".

We tend these days to think of the rapier as a feather-light weapon, the "flashing blade" of the swashbuckling heroes of the silver screen. But this is not really true. Because of their very great length – which often exceeded 1m (3.3ft) or more – and their thickened spines, most rapiers were actually very blade-heavy and somewhat ungainly in the hand.

ABOVE Key targets in rapier and dagger combat were the face and throat. A skilled swordsman could parry and attack at the same time, as shown in this early 17th-century manual by Jacques Callot (*c*.1592–1635).

BELOW Some fencing daggers had special features, such as the long down-curving guards of this Saxon dagger dating to about 1610.

The rapier was an excellent attacking weapon, but a duellist had difficulty bringing it back quickly to defend his body with a parry or blocking move. In order to attack and defend as rapidly as possible, the civilian duellist required a companion weapon. The most common was the shield, which allowed the fighter to defend himself with his left arm while attacking with his right. But shields were not convenient to carry around in daily life. An alternative was found in a weapon that people were already carrying around with them – the dagger.

By the middle of the 16th century, the dagger had become an indispensable self-defence, or "fencing", tool. The art of rapier and dagger fighting was born. The dagger was held in the left hand and used to ward off incoming attacks, leaving the rapier free to deliver lethal thrusts to the opponent's face, throat and body. The most skilled swordsman could defend himself with the dagger and attack with the rapier in a single movement. The dagger could also be used to stab the opponent if he came too close.

The *Duel des Mignons*: the advantages of a dagger

One very famous duel was fought in Paris on 27 April 1578, during the reign of Henry III (*r.*1574–89). The *mignons* (French for "favourites") were a group of obsequious young noblemen with whom the French king surrounded himself. They were known for their effeminate manners and dress, long hair and decadent, shallow lifestyle, and they became deeply unpopular with the French people. At the time of the duel, the French Court had become polarized into factions, one side supporting the king and the other side supporting his bitter rival, the Duc de Guise, a lord who enjoyed widespread popularity. The disagreement that formed the basis for the duel was said to have involved certain courtly ladies, although this may have only been a pretext.

The duel was fought between the courtiers Jacques de Quélus, who supported the king, and Charles de Balzac, Baron d'Entragues, a close ally of the Duc de Guise. Each man brought with him two companions, or seconds, and a bloody three-on-three encounter followed. One second on each side was killed outright. D'Entragues' other second died of his wounds the next day, while Quélus' other second survived with a serious head injury. The main combatants were both severely wounded. D'Entragues perhaps could be considered the victor, since he survived. Quélus suffered 19 wounds and took 33 days to die in terrible agony.

Before he died Quélus complained that the duel had been unfair, for while he had fought only with his rapier, d'Entragues had been armed with a dagger as well as his rapier. D'Entragues is said to have responded: "So much the worse for him; he ought not to have been such a fool as to have left his dagger at home."

BELOW The famous *Duel des Mignons* which was fought in Paris on 27 April 1578 during the reign of Henry III, as imagined by the 19th-century historical artist Cesare-Auguste Detti, *c.*1847.

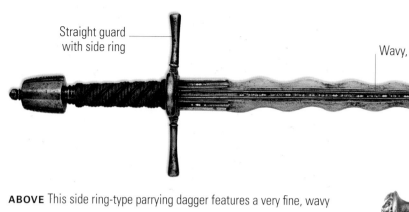

Straight guard
with side ring

Wavy, flamboyant blade

Long cross guard

Thumb depression

ABOVE This side ring-type parrying dagger features a very fine, wavy blade. The point is also specially strengthened so that it does not bend or break on contact with a harder material such as bone.

Parrying daggers

Once this new specialist use for daggers had been invented, the weapons themselves changed, becoming better suited to this particular purpose. The cross-hilt dagger was the most suitable type for fencing, since the arms of the guard offered some protection for the hand. To provide even more protection, a simple ring of metal was added to the outside of the guard. The arms of the guard were also lengthened and were often curved down towards the blade. This provided the duellist with the opportunity to ensnare his opponent's blade. If a duellist parried an attack with the lower part of his dagger blade and gave a swift twist of his wrist, his opponent's blade might become trapped between his own blade and one of the arms of the guard. His opponent's weapon might remain ensnared only for a moment, but that moment could afford the duellist the opening he required to strike a killing blow.

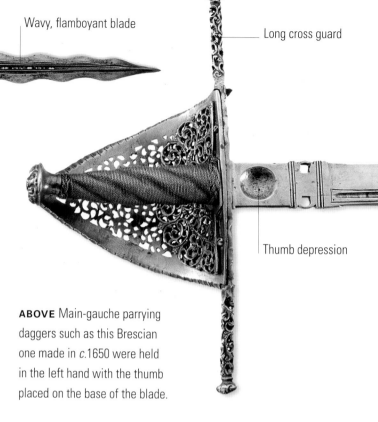

ABOVE Main-gauche parrying daggers such as this Brescian one made in *c*.1650 were held in the left hand with the thumb placed on the base of the blade.

Because of the way in which parrying daggers were used in conjunction with the rapier, they are today often called "left-hand daggers". Finer examples were made in sets with matching rapiers; sometimes the mounts and fittings of the sword belt were also decorated in the same way.

The blade of the parrying dagger tended to be somewhat longer than that of most other daggers of the time, generally being 30–45cm (12–18in) long. It was double-edged with a specially thickened ricasso that helped it resist the shock of repeated blows struck against enemy swords. It usually had a strong diamond-shaped cross-section and an even taper from guard to point. The rear side of the ricasso usually had an oval depression shaped into it. When the duellist held his dagger so that the knuckles were protected by the side ring, he would usually place his thumb on the ricasso to strengthen his parrying grip; this depression gave him better purchase on the weapon. Towards the end of the 16th century the blades of parrying daggers became more ornate and more flamboyant. They were often filed with very deep ridges and grooves running down their whole lengths. The troughs between the

LEFT *To the Death: A Sword and Dagger Fight Wherein One Hand Beats Cold Death Aside While The Other Sends It Back.* The full title of this 19th-century imagining of a rapier and dagger combat sums up the style.

ridges were frequently pierced with groups of minuscule round, square or diamond-shaped holes. Cutting deep grooves into the blade, as well as punching large numbers of tiny holes into it, reduced its weight very significantly, and it was a useful way of fine-tuning the balance of the weapon without compromising its strength or rigidity. Some blades were also given wavy edges, producing an impressive and perhaps intimidating visual effect.

Main-gauche daggers

The name of these daggers translates from the French as "left hand". Since the 19th century, English-speaking collectors have, however, used the term to refer specifically to a type of 17th-century parrying dagger that appeared in Spain and Spanish-held parts of the Low Countries and Italy. This weapon is most easily recognized by the curved, usually triangular knuckle guard extending over the hilt, the wide end of which attaches to the guard while the narrow point is affixed to the pommel. The arms of the guard are almost always very long, much longer than those found on any other form of dagger, and usually carry knob-like terminals. Main-gauche dagger pommels normally take the form of a flattened sphere, although some pommels are pear-shaped.

The blades are just as distinctive as the hilts. Some are long, narrow and double-edged, while others are single-edged and wider. The most common blade form, however, is made up of a very wide ricasso, usually pierced with a pair of large holes or sword-catching slots at the top, which then modulates into a narrow, sharply tapered section that forms the main body of the blade. In most cases these upper sections

ABOVE Later rapiers and main-gauche daggers were also made in matching sets. This handsome pair, the hilts skilfully chiselled, was made by a Neapolitan swordsmith named Antonio Cilenta in the mid-17th century.

are single-edged along the lower half of their lengths, and double-edged on the top half to the point. The back of the lower section is very often decorated with file-work along the back; similar decoration is also very often found on both edges of the ricasso section.

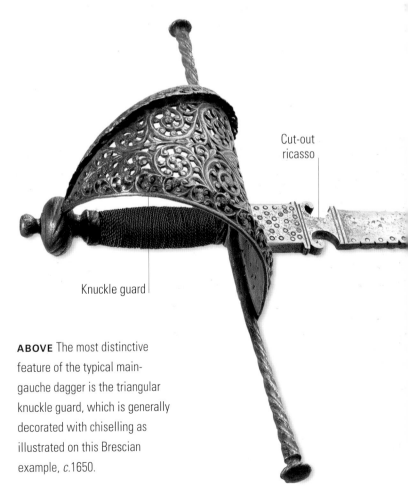

Cut-out ricasso

Knuckle guard

ABOVE The most distinctive feature of the typical main-gauche dagger is the triangular knuckle guard, which is generally decorated with chiselling as illustrated on this Brescian example, *c.*1650.

17th- and 18th-century daggers

Despite the continuing popularity of combat with both rapier and parrying dagger in Spain and Italy after 1600, the practice suffered a general decline elsewhere in Europe. Swords became lighter, smaller and quicker to deploy, and as methods of fighting with the sword alone became dominant, the dagger quickly fell out of use. Consequently, the wearing of the dagger as a fashion statement also disappeared in most places.

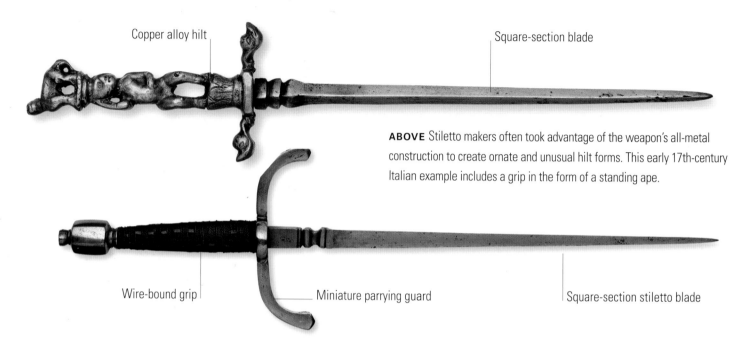

Copper alloy hilt

Square-section blade

ABOVE Stiletto makers often took advantage of the weapon's all-metal construction to create ornate and unusual hilt forms. This early 17th-century Italian example includes a grip in the form of a standing ape.

Wire-bound grip

Miniature parrying guard

Square-section stiletto blade

The elegant small sword was adopted throughout Europe almost as soon as it appeared. As well as being a brutally effective duelling weapon, its small size made it easy to carry, and its form was perfectly in tune with the mannered extravagance of the contemporary trends in art, clothing and behaviour. The carrying of daggers began to be seen as conservative or even uncivilized. By the late 17th century, daggers were distinctly out of date, surviving only as a form of localized traditionalism.

The stiletto

In the early 1600s a diminutive form of the ring-hilted parrying dagger appeared. Although it was designed in the same way as its larger cousin, with a straight or dropping cross guard and a side ring, this little weapon was too small to be used for fencing. The blade had been reduced to little more than a three- or four-sided needle of steel, and the stiletto was the result. The typical stiletto, or "stylet", of the 17th century was a very small, all-metal weapon usually measuring

ABOVE The stiletto finds its earliest origins in miniaturized parrying daggers such as this example. They were made as elegant fashion items but never meant to be used in sword fights.

20–23cm (8–9in) long. The rectangular- or triangular-section blade was very narrow, had no cutting edges and tapered to an extremely sharp point. Most of the best surviving examples are Italian and are usually exquisite demonstrations of steel cutting and chiselling. The hilt echoed the pervading fashions in architecture; the arms of the guard, grip and pommel were usually baluster-turned into undulating vase-like or bulbous shapes, and terminated in or incorporated rounded buttons, spheres and ovoid forms; the spaces between them were sometimes faceted, tapered or decorated with foliate designs in relief. Occasionally the grip and/or pommel were sculpted into the shapes of human or animal figures.

One variation was the larger gunner's stiletto. These military weapons had much longer blades, generally measuring 30–50cm (12–20in). The grip was usually

RIGHT In 1628 the commander of the English Army, George Villiers, 1st Duke of Buckingham, was stabbed to death by John Felton, a disgruntled soldier. Felton is shown here brandishing his small dagger.

made of horn, while the steel guard and pommel were often blued or blackened. The most characteristic aspect of the gunner's stiletto was the numbering on the blade. The incremental sequence varies but is most commonly 1, 3, 6, 9, 12, 14, 16, 20, 30, 40, 50, 60, 90, 100, 120. Between each number was engraved a line, which made the blade look something like a ruler.

The numbers represent the most widely used Italian artillery calibres of the time. It is therefore reasonable to assume that these daggers might originally have been designed as tools that artillerymen could use to measure the bore of a cannon, or the diameter of a cannon ball; the number corresponding to the closest line then indicated the correct weight of the ball. However, most of the surviving examples differ in the arrangement of the lines in relation to the numbering, so most would never have worked as instruments for weight calculation. They are therefore purely conventional, probably made for artillerymen as some kind of badge or status symbol. They had an impressive scientific appearance, and that was evidently more highly valued than any genuine functionality.

English cross-hilt daggers

Another of the very few distinctively 17th-century daggers appeared in England during the very early 1600s and remained popular there until at least 1675. The cross hilt of this form was comprised of a rectangular block supporting baluster-turned arms, or quillons, and usually displaying the typical English taste for foliate ornamentation in relief, which on finer examples was sometimes also encrusted in silver. Daggers of this form had no pommel. The hardwood, generally fluted grip simply swelled at the end, echoing the form of earlier ballock daggers.

The narrow blade of the 17th-century English dagger was split into three areas: a short, unsharpened ricasso of rectangular section; a middle cutting area of triangular section having a single sharpened edge, the back being characteristically serrated like a saw; and a reinforced stabbing point of diamond section. The ricasso and mid-section are often etched with heads in profile, scrolling vegetation and mottos, and many examples are also dated.

BELOW English daggers of the 17th century are easily recognized by their characteristic hilts and heavily etched blades, many of which are dated like this example, which is marked 1628.

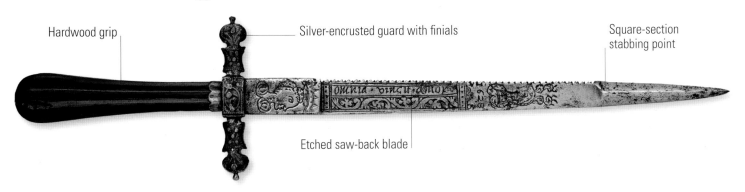

Hardwood grip — Silver-encrusted guard with finials — Square-section stabbing point

Etched saw-back blade

RIGHT Typical "Mediterranean" dirks such as this one made in the second half of the 18th century in Liguria, northwestern Italy, have very wide bases waisting into narrow tangs.

Locket

Chape

Grooved handle

Ricasso decorated with rooster

Double fuller

"Mediterranean" dirks

A third important group of daggers appeared along the north coast of the Mediterranean in the mid-1600s. The weapons, collectively referred to as "Mediterranean" dirks, were actually made in a wide range of sizes and display an extraordinary variety of ornament.

The one-piece handle, made of wood, ivory or horn, is always bored through its centre to accept the narrow tang of the blade; the end is capped with metal, often silver, and the end of the tang peened (hammered) over to secure the blade. The handle in most cases also swells slightly away from the blade. "Mediterranean" dirks almost never have any form of guard. The top of the handle is generally covered with a metal sleeve or protective band at the bottom of the hilt called a

ferrule, which modulates upwards into the blade via a short post, called the root of the blade. This is usually turned or faceted in a similar manner to, although stouter than, the balustered forms found on stilettos of the same period.

"Mediterranean" dirks carry either single- or double-edged blades. The single-edged types usually have a deep, unsharpened section called a choil dropping down from the handle in the manner of most kitchen knives. Usually the choil is straight, although in some cases it takes a graceful recurved line. The double-edged Mediterranean blade resembles a broad spearhead, with rounded shoulders at the base. Generally the edges of both types do not taper in straight lines but rather bulge slightly like a very

Braided leather sheath

Claw handle

Sheath fringe

ABOVE This Native American fighting knife incorporates a European "butcher" knife blade of the 18th or early 19th century, having a straight unsharpened back and curved cutting edge.

Scalping

One practice closely associated with the darker aspects of the frontier experience in North America during the 17th, 18th and 19th centuries was scalping. This brutal exercise in mutilation involved the victim being pinned down to the ground on his or her chest, with one of the attacker's knees or feet placed between the shoulder blades. The head was yanked up by the hair and a deep incision cut all the way around the hairline with a long fighting knife. A swift tug on the handful of hair tore the skin from the skull like a bloody rag.

The scalping of dead enemies was a rare form of trophy-taking in battle among certain Native American tribes before the arrival of Europeans. It had also been practised intermittently in Europe for thousands of years. But it was encouraged on an unprecedented scale in North America after the arrival of European colonists, and was practised by white men as well as native peoples, on living as well as dead victims. In the late 17th century, scalping was endorsed by both sides during the Anglo-French conflicts that played out for nearly 100 years across what is now the United States

RIGHT This French 18th-century lithograph depicts an Iroquois warrior scalping a bound captive. He is in the process of pulling the scalp off while applying pressure with his right foot.

and Canada. The French began paying for British scalps in the 1680s, and the British reciprocated by offering as much as £100 (about £8,000 today) for French and Indian scalps in the 1690s.

shallow arch. Most single-edged varieties are also sharpened on the top a few centimetres off the back. Most good examples are decorated at the base of the blade with relief ornament, engraving and piercings.

American "butcher" and "scalping" knives

The fighting knives carried on the North American frontier were quite different from the ornate daggers made in Europe, being plainer, cruder and designed to work well for a much wider range of uses – fighting men and wild animals but also undertaking the daily tasks associated with living in the forests and mountains of the frontier. The large size of these knives can be inferred from descriptions of soldiers joining the American Army in 1775, who, we are told, carried "butcher" or "scalping" knives. Because they were

simply made by local craftsmen according to individual preference, they are almost impossible to date precisely, and very little else can be said about them for certain.

Despite these difficulties, it is possible to identify two basic knife forms typically carried by Americans in the 18th century. One was essentially a cross-hilt dagger with a stout double-edged blade, short guard and wooden grip that was simply tapped in place around the tang. The second was single-edged, usually with a slight curve to the back and a shallow choil above the grip. As with contemporary "Mediterranean" dirks, these American weapons looked very much like utilitarian knives, and undoubtedly this similarity led to them being described as "butcher" knives. Given the brutal use to which these knives were put, by all sides in the North American wars, it is an apt description.

Scottish dirks

The 17th century brought with it a rapid decline in the evolution and use of traditional daggers in most parts of Europe. But in a few more isolated areas, the practice of wearing and fighting with the dagger continued unabated. In northern Europe the persistent development of the essentially medieval weapon is most noticeable in Scotland, where, sometime in the 17th century, one of the most iconic daggers of all time appeared.

The four important members of the medieval family of daggers experienced quite divergent later histories. The basic cross-hilted dagger multiplied into a number of more specialized forms in the 16th and 17th centuries, including the assorted forms of parrying dagger, stiletto and English dagger of the 1600s. The baselard was transformed into the classic "Swiss" dagger before disappearing by 1600. The rondel dagger, which had been such an essential part of the armoured warrior's arsenal, became scarcer as warfare became modernized and hand-to-hand combat between men-at-arms declined. The last of the great medieval dagger forms, the ballock, died out everywhere in Europe except in Scotland, where it evolved into two important new forms.

The dudgeon dagger
In the first quarter of the 17th century the earlier of the two Scottish derivatives of the medieval ballock dagger appeared in Lowland Scotland. It was generally called a "dagger of dudgeon" or simply "dudgeon

ABOVE This early 17th-century dudgeon dagger shows clearly its descent from earlier ballock daggers of the 15th and 16th centuries. It retains its cutting edges, but the thick spine makes it primarily a stabbing weapon.

dagger". The 17th-century term "dudgeon" referred to the hardwood that was used to fashion the hilt. A single piece of hardwood, most commonly boxwood but also ebony, ivy root and others, was carved into a particular interpretation of the distinctive ballock hilt design. The lobes below the base of the blade were generally quite small and much less bulbous than their medieval forebears, and were often decorated with little copper-alloy or silver rosettes on the top of each lobe. These rosettes were actually washers supporting rivets that held in place a crescent-shaped iron or steel spacer seated on the base of the blade between it and the top of the hilt. The grip swelled towards its top end, but again not in so obvious a

BELOW Dudgeon daggers display very fine etched decoration on their blades, frequently involving scrolling foliage as seen here.

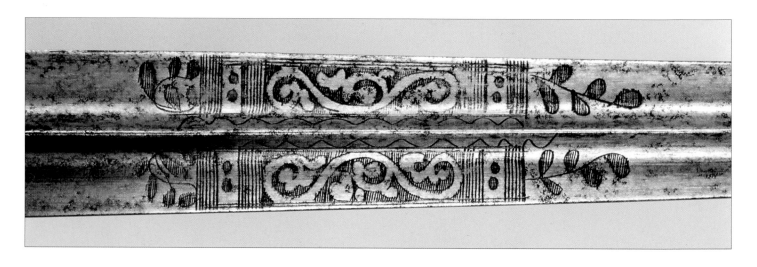

Etched and gilt blade

Dudgeon handle

Metal chape

Open-work locket

ABOVE This very fine dudgeon dagger in a private collection may have belonged to François Ravaillac, murderer of King Henry IV of France. It is undoubtedly Scottish; the scabbard appears to be later European work.

way as earlier forms of ballock dagger. The grip was usually faceted and bored out for the tang of the blade; the end of the tang, where it protruded from the top of the grip, was generally covered with a metal button.

The long, narrow blade is the most instantly recognizable part of the dudgeon dagger, for despite each of the surviving examples being unique, the blades are all obviously of a type. They taper evenly from base to point and are almost always of a strong diamond (almost square) section, the sides being deeply hollow-ground. Occasionally this shaping is taken to an extreme degree, producing a blade that is essentially flat but which carries a very thick medial ridge. Sometimes the section is varied within zones along the length of the blade; one of these multi-section blades might begin with a typical rectangular-section ricasso, modulating to a hollow-ground diamond-section zone a few centimetres or so up the blade, then giving way to a single-edged area and finally ending with a square-section stabbing point.

Dudgeon dagger blades are always etched with scrolling vines and leafy patterns. Some also carry mottos or invocations. Some are dated, the dates always falling between 1600 and 1625, although it is certain that they were fashionable for a longer period. In 1635 the soldier, politician and writer Sir William Brereton wrote that on a visit to Edinburgh he bought "a dudgeon-hafted dagger … gilt". All known dudgeon dagger blades are (or were) fire-gilt over their entire surfaces, the gold combining with the etching to give the weapons a very rich appearance.

Several other notable figures in the 17th century owned dudgeon daggers. One is said to have belonged to François Ravaillac (1578–1610), the Catholic zealot who stabbed to death King Henry IV of France (1553–1610). Another was confiscated from Colonel Thomas Blood (1618–1680) after his failed attempt to steal the Crown Jewels of England in 1671.

LEFT This portrait of François Ravaillac commemorates him as the royal assassin of Henry IV. The artist has chosen to depict him grasping a dudgeon dagger with a wavy, flamboyant blade.

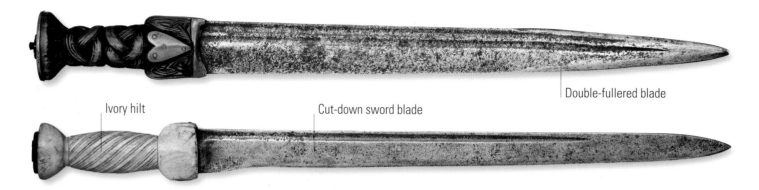

Double-fullered blade

Ivory hilt

Cut-down sword blade

The Highland dirk

The success of the dudgeon dagger kept the ballock dagger alive in Scotland after it had vanished everywhere else in Europe. While the dudgeon dagger was primarily carried in the Lowlands, as well as finding its way to a limited degree to England and the Continent, it may also have made an impression on the Gaelic-speaking Highlanders in the northwest of Scotland. The Highlanders still fought in an essentially medieval way, with swords, round shields and staff weapons. It may not have been long before a few dudgeon daggers fell into the hands of some of the richer clan warriors. Copies were made bigger and longer, better suited to use on the battlefield. By 1650 the Highland dirk had been created.

A number of features connect the Highland dirk and the earlier dudgeon dagger. Highland craftsmen generally used their own type of "dudgeon", namely bogwood, for the construction of the hilt. Bogwood was taken from ancient trees that had been submerged in the local peat bogs for thousands of years. The wood that was used to make dirk hilts, usually oak, was partially fossilized and consequently very hard – perfect for the purpose and easily accessible.

Dirk hilts were also cast in solid brass or, more rarely, carved in bone. They also generally displayed the spacers between blade and hilt observed on the earlier

TOP The bogwood hilts of Highland dirks like this one from around 1740 were often decorated with brass plaques or plates. Sometimes the whole hilt would be made of solid brass.

ABOVE This 18th-century dirk is fitted with a less common type of hilt, carved in ivory. Bone was also occasionally used. Here a single piece of ivory has been cut and filed to create a very attractive spiralled grip.

dudgeon daggers, along with a more stylized version of the ballock hilt. The lobes were much subtler, sometimes becoming flattened against the sides of the grip. Only an echo, if anything, of their original inspiration was suggested in the carving of the hilt, which was now covered in intricate knotwork designs. The pommel was flattened and widened into a disk shape, undoubtedly to provide a better grip in battle, and usually covered with a metal cap.

Highland dirk blades could be either single- or double-edged. Single-edged examples tended to be very broad at the ricasso and tapered evenly to a sharp point. The thick back of the single-edged dirk blade was often decorated with file marks or serrations and emphasized

BELOW Decorated dress dirks were produced in large numbers from the 19th century. This silver-mounted example made in Edinburgh in c.1900 has a small byknife and fork contained in special scabbard sleeves.

Fork

Byknife

Silver locket

Basket-weave carving

by a fuller running parallel just inside of it. Frequently, the back only extended two thirds of the way towards the point, the last third being double-edged. Other blades were entirely double-edged; indeed it was not uncommon for them to be fashioned out of old or broken sword blades.

Dirk blades were generally very long, some measuring 46cm (18in) or more. Like their medieval ancestors, they were used to stab overarm, with the blade below the fist. When the Highland warrior was fully armed, with his sword in his right hand and his *targe* (shield) in his left, the dirk was sometimes also grasped in the left hand. If enough of the blade extended below the edge of the shield, the dirk could be used offensively in that position, or passed to the right hand if the sword was lost.

After 1750 the Highland dirk began to change, shifting from a traditional weapon used by people living an ancient lifestyle into a somewhat gaudy showpiece. It became a signature badge of the Highland regiments of the British Army and the essential features became exaggerated. The grip began to be studded with small round-headed nails and bulged much more drastically in its midst, taking on an exaggerated thistle shape. In the 19th century the craze for all things Scottish turned the Highland dirk into a parody of itself, the carving of the hilt degenerating into second-rate basketwork, the scabbards set with hulking silver or gilt mounts, and the whole object finished off with large yellow crystals called cairngorms (or more often, glass imitations). This modern version, much removed from the original form, remains a standard part of formal Highland dress.

The sgian dubh (skean dhu)

Another small Scottish knife that should be mentioned at this point, although it is really a 19th-century creation, is the *sgian dubh* (*skean dhu*), or "black knife". Like the later Highland dirk, this very small knife is still worn as part of Highland dress. While this weapon may be a descendant of knives carried by Highland warriors, there are no surviving examples that date from earlier than the 19th century. It is therefore generally thought, probably correctly, that the sgian dubh was a product of the Romantic revival of Highland dress in the 1800s.

RIGHT The famous sgian dubh may be descended from small knives hidden up the sleeve, but in their well-known form they are entirely modern and cosmetic, as is this early 20th-century Edinburgh-made example.

Silver spacer

Silver scabbard chape

LEFT The *c*.1870 portrait of John Chisholm of the Clan Chisholm (factions of which fought on both sides at the Battle of Culloden) shows Highland dress complete with the long dirk worn on the right side and the sgian dubh down the right stocking.

17th- and 18th-century bayonets

Early long-guns were one-shot weapons. After firing, they took time to reload. In that time an enemy could rush the shooter to attack him at close-quarters. The shooter could defend himself with an empty musket by swinging it like a club, but this required space to move – an uncommon luxury in pitched battle. The invention of the bayonet made it possible to transform the musket into a short spear, perfect for close combat.

Bone/ivory handle — Decorative cross-guard finials — Dagger-type blade

It is remarkable that so soon after the enormous technological breakthrough that was the hand-held firearm, men were searching for a way to turn it back into one of humanity's most ancient weapons – a spear. Until the mid-17th century, the spear and the firearm worked together – an army's musketeers were protected by ranks of soldiers armed with long spears called pikes. The pikemen formed a hedge-like defence, which kept the enemy from rushing the musketeers while they reloaded. But this meant that any man with a pike was restricted to an entirely defensive role. This was wasteful and military theorists worked hard to find a way to give the musketeer defensive as well as offensive capabilities. Initial efforts were not very successful. One idea was for the musketeer to unscrew the head of his musket-rest and then insert the long staff into the barrel of his musket, turning it into a spear. But this process was quickly found to be slow and troublesome.

The birth of the bayonet

It is not known when and from whom the inspiration of wedding a knife to the end of a musket first came, but it is likely to have happened in or near Eibar in the Basque province of Guipúzcoa, northwestern Spain. Eibar was an important centre for the production of weapons during the late 16th century, an industry that was also the economic mainstay of many surrounding towns. It is possible that daggers designed for wedging into the muzzles of long-guns

ABOVE This English plug bayonet of the late 17th century shows a very fine inlaid handle. It is fitted with a decorated pommel cap and an ornately wrought cross guard.

were being produced here as early as the 1580s, probably for hunters. Like the soldiers of the time, hunters were armed with single-shot firearms and were in danger of being charged by their wounded prey; they thus had to be protected by another man with a spear. A knife jammed quickly into the barrel of the long-gun allowed a man to hunt alone. It would not be long before the military potential of this invention was realized.

The daggers of Bayonne

This specialized dagger, which would later become universally known as the "bayonet", initially referred to any dagger made in Bayonne in the southwestern corner of France, not far from Eibar. It may have been first employed in battle during the French Wars of Religion (1562–1629). At the Battle of Ivry in 1590, King Henry IV of France is said to have armed his troops with bayonets. Henry himself came from the Basque region where the bayonet was probably developed and at the time of the battle he did not have enough pikemen. The musket-dagger from his native land would have been an excellent solution to this problem. Voltaire (1694–1778), the great French dramatist and satirist, certainly believed that King Henry's men had bayonets at Ivry. In reference to

what turned out to be Henry's great victory, Voltaire in 1723 wrote one of the most evocative descriptions of this new weapon:

United with the musket, the bloody knife
Already for both sides posed a double death.
This weapon which once, to depopulate the earth,
In Bayonne was invented by the demon of war
Mustered simultaneously, those worthy fruits of Hell,
Which are most terrible, the fire and the steel.

The city of Bayonne had also produced edged weapons during the 16th century. The earliest known use of the term "bayonet" describes "a gilded dagger which was given the name Bayonnet". A French-English dictionary of 1611 defines the word as "a kind of small flat pocket dagger… or a great knife to hang at the girdle". Other sources mention daggers "of Bayonne". It seems that these weapons did not differ very greatly from other common types of daggers. Yet once the idea of the bayonet (as it is now understood) had taken off, Bayonne could have become the first manufacturer of the weapon on a large scale. It would not therefore be surprising if such a precise term as "bayonet", a word that lacked an equally unambiguous meaning, were to have gained a more exact use in the application to this newly specialized weapon.

ABOVE *The Battle of Ivry*, by Peter Paul Rubens, *c.*1628–1630. Henry IV's famous victory on 14 March 1590 over the Catholic League is said to have been the first time the bayonet was deployed as a battlefield weapon.

BELOW Musketeers had to be protected when reloading. Here they are marching alongside halberdiers, although pikemen were commonly used to guard them on the battlefield until the introduction of the bayonet.

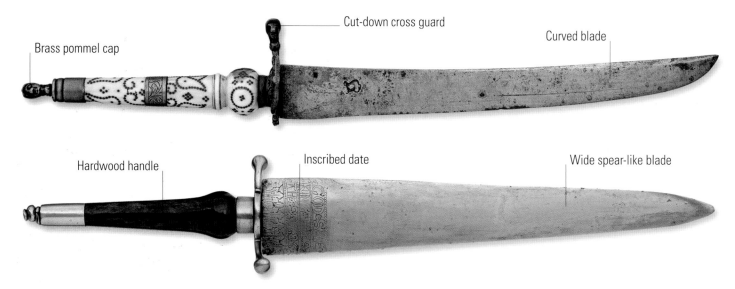

Brass pommel cap

Cut-down cross guard

Curved blade

Hardwood handle

Inscribed date

Wide spear-like blade

Plug bayonets

An important early reference to the military bayonet was made by Jacques de Chastenet (1600–1682), a French commander and native of Bayonne. In a description of the soldiers under his command in 1647, he wrote:

…they had bayonets with handles one foot long, and the blades of the bayonets were as long as the handles, the ends of which were adapted for putting in the barrels of the muskets to defend themselves, when attacked after they had fired.

This passage is not only the first reliable source that places the bayonet in a military context, it is also the first definite use of the term "bayonet" in reference to an edged weapon designed to be inserted into the barrel of a firearm. De Chastenet is discussing what we now call a "plug bayonet", essentially a dagger with a tapered grip that can be jammed firmly into the firing end or muzzle of a musket.

Although undoubtedly an important innovation, the plug bayonet was not without its drawbacks. Once embedded in an enemy, it could be hard to withdraw without it popping out of the barrel, making repeated attacks very difficult. More crucially, the musket could not be fired with the bayonet in place. This weakness of the design had serious consequences. At the Battle of Killiecrankie (1689) the British Army was defeated by the Jacobites, mostly Highland Scots, because their musketeers had to pause to fix bayonets. The Jacobites therefore wisely employed the famous "Highland Charge". After firing the few firearms that they had, the Jacobites rushed downhill into the British line armed with swords and shields. While this tactic meant that the Jacobites received a full barrage of musket fire

TOP English bladesmiths initially experimented with curved bayonet blades, such as this one dated 1680, but they were soon abandoned.

ABOVE This slightly later example of an English bayonet, dated 1686, is more typical in form, having a blade that is not dissimilar to the wide spearheads of previous centuries.

BELOW French military scientist Sébastien Le Prestre, Seigneur de Vauban, developed the socket bayonet as a response to the plug bayonet's debilitating drawback of preventing fire while being fixed. His work revolutionized early modern warfare.

LE MARÉCHAL
DE VAUBAN.

as they raced in, those that survived were suddenly amongst their enemies before bayonets could be fixed. At such close range, the swords and shields of the Jacobites outclassed those redcoats who had managed to put their bayonets to use. The British forces were cut to pieces, suffering over 2000 casualties.

The socket bayonet

A number of plug bayonet modifications were considered as ways of getting around the essential firing problem. The "ring bayonet" is often thought to have been one of these modifications, wherein a pair of rings was used to fix the bayonet to the side of the musket barrel. There is, however, no evidence that ring bayonets actually existed beyond the drawing board. Another short-lived idea was the "folding bayonet"– a thin, spear-like projection permanently attached to the barrel, which hinged into place.

The plug bayonet was made obsolete by the invention of the socket bayonet. This new form was composed of a tubular sleeve that fitted over the end of the musket's barrel, to the side of which was welded a bayonet blade. The famous military scientist Sébastien Le Prestre, Seigneur de Vauban (1633–1707), was the most active early developer of the socket bayonet, if not its inventor. In 1687 he wrote that as a result of the adoption of the socket bayonet:

…a soldier with a single weapon would have two of the best in the world in his hand… he could fire and reload very quickly without removing the bayonet. By doing this, there is no doubt that a batallion armed in this way…would be worth at least two of any existing batallions and would be in a position to scorn the pikes and the cavalry of any country…

De Vauban advocated a bayonet blade that was triangular in section, with one flat side facing against the barrel. The earliest socket bayonets had blades

ABOVE King Frederick II of Prussia (1712–1786), called "the Great", was one of the greatest military leaders of all time. This 19th-century lithograph shows him at the head of his army, which bristles with bayonets.

welded directly to the socket, but this was not ideal as slightly bent blades could project into the bullet's path. They also made muzzle loading difficult; a musketeer might accidentally stab himself in the hand while ramming down a charge. To improve the design, the blade was placed on the end of a short arm, or shank, which projected out and away from the line of fire, placing the blade along its own parallel path.

Although a great many slight adjustments to this bayonet concept were to come, the essential idea proved so successful that this remained the standard bayonet form for nearly 200 years. Thus what was really a late 17th-century piece of technology was still in use during World War I, and was even reintroduced by the British Army during World War II.

BELOW Some early socket bayonets such as this 18th-century example had wide blades like the earlier plug versions, but were supported by an L-shaped bracket and socket.

Mortise

Shell-guard

19th-century edged weapons

The Industrial Revolution ushered in the mass production of weapons. Knives and daggers continued to be made by hand but traditional bladesmiths were less essential. The use of fighting knives for personal defence declined dramatically in Europe, but less so in the United States. Mass production made it possible to standardize bayonet manufacture, and millions of duplicates of pattern types were produced for every major world army.

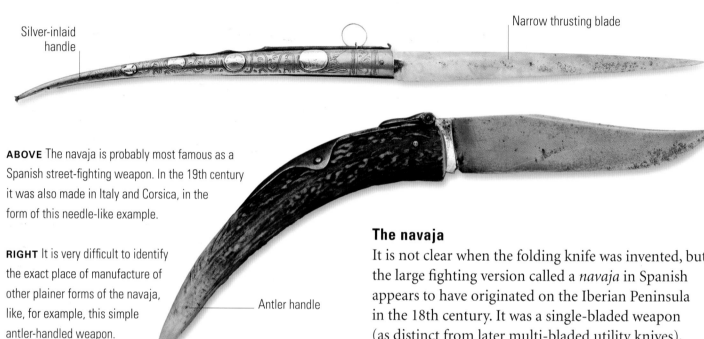

Silver-inlaid handle

Narrow thrusting blade

Antler handle

ABOVE The navaja is probably most famous as a Spanish street-fighting weapon. In the 19th century it was also made in Italy and Corsica, in the form of this needle-like example.

RIGHT It is very difficult to identify the exact place of manufacture of other plainer forms of the navaja, like, for example, this simple antler-handled weapon.

In the first half of the 19th century, most European countries were establishing professional police forces charged with keeping the public peace. Law and order became an expected part of everyday civilian life, and personal violence became increasingly unacceptable. The fashion for men to carry knives and daggers as a matter of routine fell away rapidly as the sense of a need for public decorum and civility prevailed in the minds of law-abiding people. An important exception to this general social trend was the recently formed United States of America.

Knives in the United States

In the first half of the 19th century most American men wore knives. The seemingly marked increase in the practice during the 1820s and 1830s, in direct contrast to European developments, was perhaps due to the increasing social discord that later culminated in the American Civil War (1861–65). During these turbulent decades, several key knife-types stood out.

The navaja

It is not clear when the folding knife was invented, but the large fighting version called a *navaja* in Spanish appears to have originated on the Iberian Peninsula in the 18th century. It was a single-bladed weapon (as distinct from later multi-bladed utility knives), the blade having a clipped point and usually being 15–20cm (6–8in) long, although some extended to 30cm (1ft) or even more. The blade was locked open by means of a spring catch. To release it, one usually pulled up on a ring or chain to free the catch and release the blade, which could then be closed again. The narrow grip, which could be straight although most were curved, was usually made up of an iron lining decorated with stag or cow horn. More expensive examples were ornamented with ivory and sometimes even gold.

The navaja was known as the weapon of workers, criminals and sailors. It was made in France, Italy and Corsica as well as Spain. In 1849, a manual on navaja fighting techniques was published in Madrid; it also contained instruction on how to fight with other knives and with scissors.

In North America the navaja is also considered a classic fighting knife, especially in California where no doubt this particular weapon was one of the many legacies of former Spanish rule. The navaja must have been common in the streets of old San Francisco,

which appears to have been an especially violent place in the mid-19th century. One account describes a lawman being stabbed by a judge, although whether or not he used a navaja is not mentioned.

The push dagger

Another classic American weapon of the early 19th century was the push dagger. This deadly little weapon was composed of a stout double-edged blade with a short, round-section tang that terminated in a transverse grip – of bone, horn or wood – giving the dagger an overall T-shape. A man would grip a push dagger in his fist with the blade protruding between the middle and ring fingers, the base of the blade sitting a little less than 2.5cm (1in) above the knuckles. He would strike a blow with a swift punching movement; bystanders might not even be aware that a knife attack had occurred, nor even the victim until he caught sight of his own blood.

The push dagger scabbard was often made to be worn upside-down inside a coat or jacket, having a spring clip to retain the weapon and a hook on the end of the chape for suspension. In this way a man could easily secrete a push dagger about his person and draw it quickly when the need arose. Almost all surviving examples (before their re-emergence in the 20th century) seem to date from before around 1860.

ABOVE This portrait of James Bowie (1793–1836) was probably completed in the late 1820s, around the time he and his brother Rezin were perfecting their famous knife.

ABOVE The 1836 storming of the Alamo mission by Mexican troops. James Bowie died during the battle, purportedly defending himself from his sickbed with firearms and his knife.

The Bowie knife

In 1827 an Arkansas plantation owner named Rezin Pleasant Bowie was attacked by a bull. Rezin tried to stab the bull in the head, but his knife could not pierce the bull's skull. Rezin managed to survive nonetheless, and in his quest for a more reliable knife he had an old file ground down to create a large single-edged knife. The blade was over 23cm (9in) long and 4cm (1.5in) wide, and it was fitted with a cross guard and simple wooden grip. Rezin gave a knife of this form to his brother James, who later that same year was involved in the famous "sandbar fight" at Vidalia, Louisiana, on the Mississippi River. James was shot and stabbed, but still managed to use his brother's knife to disembowel one assailant, wound another and chase off a third. The local press reported the fight, along with details of James Bowie's unusually large knife, and a legend began.

"Jim" Bowie's fame increased in 1829 when he wounded and then spared a man in a knife fight. That episode in itself would perhaps not have proved newsworthy but for the fact that shortly thereafter Bowie was attacked by three associates of his defeated opponent. He apparently decapitated one and disembowelled another. The third fled.

The knife that Jim Bowie used in 1829 was a new version that he had commissioned himself, a modification of his brother Rezin's original idea. The weapon had a longer blade with a clipped point sharpened on both sides. This design became the basis for the traditional Bowie knife, as it is known today.

In 1830 Jim Bowie moved to Texas and became involved in the local rebellion against Mexican rule. After numerous battles, he ended up at the siege of the Alamo in 1836. One hundred and eighty-eight Texans defended this small mission complex against an overwhelming Mexican force. When the Mexicans stormed the mission, the Texans killed at least 200 and wounded another 400 before being wiped out. Bowie was ill in bed during the final assault; nevertheless, he is said to have defended himself with his pistols, a broken rifle and his famous knife before being killed.

After this last battle, it seemed that everyone wanted a Bowie knife, even if nobody could agree on what it was supposed to look like. Clearly it needed to have a

BELOW The English manufacturer James Rodgers & Co produced a number of different types of Bowie knife for the American market in the years immediately before the American Civil War. This Rodgers "medium" includes an antler grip.

Spherical guard terminal

Clipped point

Antler grip

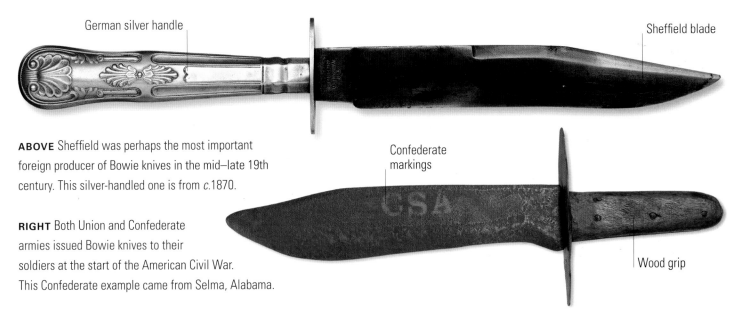

German silver handle

Sheffield blade

ABOVE Sheffield was perhaps the most important foreign producer of Bowie knives in the mid–late 19th century. This silver-handled one is from *c.*1870.

Confederate markings

Wood grip

RIGHT Both Union and Confederate armies issued Bowie knives to their soldiers at the start of the American Civil War. This Confederate example came from Selma, Alabama.

big blade and there was a general consensus that it should be single-edged. Soon the name "Bowie knife" was used to refer to any large single-edged knife. They began to be manufactured in Mississippi, Louisiana, Arkansas, Texas, Tennessee and Missouri. The blades were 23–38cm (9–15in) long and generally 4–5cm (1.5–2in) wide. The guards were straight or S-shaped, while grips were usually made of wood or antler. Many Bowie knives were also customized and personalized by their owners in some way.

English cutlery manufacturers quickly realized the potential of this product and began exporting it in large numbers for sale to hunters, trappers, soldiers and others in the harsh environment of the American frontier. As more Bowie knives became available, firms began to compete by producing more elaborate and expensive versions. Mother-of-pearl and turtle-shell grips were mounted on silver hilts, while blades were acid-etched and even blued and gilt. English makers also emblazoned them with jingoistic slogans conceived to appeal to Americans at the time, such as "Death to Traitors" (hinting at rising pre-Civil War tensions), "Death to Abolition" (appealing to the predominant southern demand for the continuation of slavery), and "Equal Rights and Justice for All" (representing the northern stance against slavery).

At the beginning of the American Civil War, the Bowie knife was popular on both sides, the Confederates favouring a version fitted with a D-shaped knuckle guard. This initial popularity in a way mirrored the original passion for the war in both the Union and Confederate States, and just like that enthusiasm, it died out as the conflict became longer and bloodier. By the end of the war both North and South had discarded their fighting knives, and after peace was declared the wearing of knives became distinctly unfashionable. By 1880, the true Bowie knife had disappeared.

LEFT Bowie knives were popular with trappers, mountain men and cowboys. Here the famous gunfighter James Butler "Wild Bill" Hickok (1837–1876) is photgraphed with two revolvers and a long Bowie knife.

"Zigzag" slot

The socket bayonet

This bayonet remained the primary type issued to the rank-and-file soldier throughout most of the 19th century. While blade forms varied to some extent, the main area of improvement in the 1800s was the method of attachment. In the 18th century the most common method had been a "zigzag" slot in the socket, which engaged with the forward sight and locked with a half turn. This method was not entirely satisfactory. At the battle of Meeanee, during the Indian Sind campaign of 1843, British soldiers encountered problems when their enemies started pulling the bayonets off in combat, requiring them to be tied on more securely with string. British arms manufacturers were meanwhile experimenting with new spring mechanisms to lock the bayonet down more securely.

Spring catch

The spring bayonet

The Hanoverian spring catch came into service in the same year as Meeanee. This little S-shaped catch, fitted to the barrel, engaged a collar on the bayonet and made it more difficult to be dislodged. The locking ring was an even better idea, and was quickly taken up by France and other European countries. The locking ring allowed the sight to seat down into the socket slot through a notch at its join, but then was rotated to lock behind the sight. Britain adopted the locking ring in 1853, when it was fitted to the Enfield rifle bayonet.

The sword bayonet

Late in the 18th century, in Denmark, attempts were made to create two weapons in one when the 1791 cavalry sword was converted into a bayonet by shortening the blade and fitting an attachment mechanism to the side of the weapon. The British married similar long "sword" bayonets to the 1800 Baker and 1837 Brunswick rifles. The French introduced perhaps the most popular sword

Hollow-ground blade

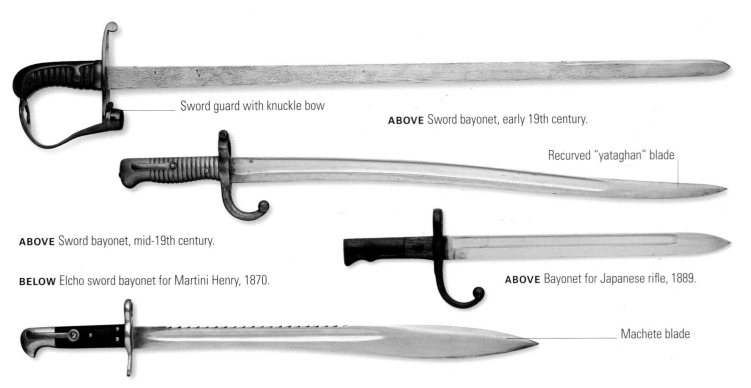

Sword guard with knuckle bow

ABOVE Sword bayonet, early 19th century.

Recurved "yataghan" blade

ABOVE Sword bayonet, mid-19th century.

BELOW Elcho sword bayonet for Martini Henry, 1870.

ABOVE Bayonet for Japanese rifle, 1889.

Machete blade

RIGHT Francis Richard Charteris, Lord Elcho, 10th Earl of Wemyss, was a prominent Whig politician, commander of the London Scottish Regiment, and inventor of the Elcho bayonet. He died at the age of 96 in 1914.

bayonet pattern in 1842. It had a brass hilt, simple cross guard, and a beaked pommel. The recurved "yataghan" blade-shape was taken from the famous Turkish sword. It was enormously successful and adopted in Scandinavia, Austria, Britain, the United States and many other countries. The British 1853 and 1856 artillery bayonets were carbon-copies of the French 1842, while in the United States various yataghan-bladed bayonets appeared; these included the 1855 and 1861 (Navy) patterns.

The sword bayonet remained popular until the late 19th century despite being heavy and impractical, and a large number of sword designs proliferated after 1850. Britain took the lead, developing many versions in the ultimately futile search for a multi-use weapon. Cutlass bayonets were issued to the Navy and knuckle-guard types developed for artillerymen. One of the oddest was Lord Elcho's "1870 experimental sword bayonet", which was also a sword, saw and machete. The Elcho suffered from the flaw inherent in all combination weapons – any attempt to design for multiple uses always compromises each of those uses. It was very expensive to manufacture and its heaviness made shooting difficult. Initially rejected, the Elcho was revived in 1895 and saw limited use in the Ashanti campaign of 1895–6.

The long and complicated exercise of developing the sword bayonet was proved to be ultimately futile, being the wrong weapon for a rapidly modernizing battlefield. Artillery and overall firepower superiority were the keys to modern war, and the bayonet was essentially a defensive weapon of last resort. Sword versions were consequently discarded in favour of smaller knife types. In 200 years the bayonet, which had begun its history as a knife jammed into the muzzle, had returned to its roots.

20th-century edged weapons

Advances in firearms technology, and the soldier's increased individual firepower created by the widespread adoption of bolt-action magazine rifles by the early years of the 20th century, reduced the chances of close contact with the enemy. However, bayonets and fighting knives still maintained their place in the soldier's armoury, whether as weapons on the battlefield or ceremonial items on the parade ground.

During the early years of the 20th century, warfare underwent its most dramatic changes since the appearance of the firearm. At sea vast increases in naval firepower meant that battleships now engaged at ranges of miles rather than yards. Boarding parties wielding cutlasses and axes were becoming a distant memory and submarines added a new dimension as stalking assassins. Warfare took to the air, at first tentatively and then in earnest, allowing death to be dealt from above and taking conflict beyond the battlefield to the towns and cities of the enemy. Land warfare also underwent dramatic change. New types of artillery meant that it outranked every other weapon on the battlefield. When joined by the machine gun both had a devastating impact on the way battles were fought. The days of stalemate entrenchment dawned with World War I (1914–18). When the idea emerged of placing artillery and machine guns in armour-plated, fast-moving vehicles, entrenchment gave way to "Blitzkrieg" – lightning war – in World War II (1939–45).

But technology tends to advance faster than the abilities of soldiers to integrate it into new tactics and strategies effectively, especially if they have been tutored in the "old ways". Although long sword bayonets and battlefield derring-do such as cavalry and bayonet charges had been rendered ineffective by the late 19th century, a surprisingly long time had to pass before this equipment and such practices were finally discarded in favour of equipment and tactics more suited to the needs of the tasks in hand.

Bayonets of World War I

Despite the fact that in the late 19th century long sword bayonets had been found to be too cumbersome and awkward to be really effective, most nations retained them as they entered World War I. The old idea of "reach" – the ability to outreach the enemy's rifle with a bayonet attached – persisted. Austro-Hungarian infantrymen were issued with the 1895 Mannlicher 8mm rifle which was fitted with a long sword bayonet. The Turks, carrying the Mauser Gewehr 98 7.65mm rifle, also preferred a very long-bladed bayonet with a cross guard, which had a hook-shaped quillon. Whether used to allow rifles to be stacked together neatly in a tripod arrangement or, as some would believe, to ensnare the enemy's bayonet blade and either break it or deflect the thrust, these bayonets were still far more likely to become snagged on something inconsequential

RIGHT An illustration of a French bayonet charge at Valmy featured on the front page of this French newspaper in 1915.

BELOW The optimistic French bayonet charges of the first half of World War I employed the long needle-bladed Lebel bayonet like this pre-1916 example.

Narrow hollow-ground blade

All-metal grip

ABOVE This rare black-and-white photo of the 10th Company of the 9th Russian Guards, taken in 1917, shows the Russian troops armed with old-fashioned socket bayonets.

at a crucial moment. The Italian bayonets for the Mannlicher-Carcano and Vetterli-Carcano rifles of the late 19th century which saw service in World War I resembled the British 1907 Pattern.

The British, who had discarded their various long sword bayonets in favour of the shorter knife patterns of 1888 and 1903, returned before World War I to a long-bladed sword bayonet design, the 1907 Pattern, which replaced the 1903 Pattern on their SMLE (Short, Magazine, Lee-Enfield) rifles. The 1907 Pattern, which was equipped with a 43cm (17in) blade, was produced initially with a cross guard featuring a "hook" quillon, reflecting widespread 19th-century fashion. The design was very successful; basically copied from the Japanese Model 1897 Arisaka bayonet, more than 2.5 million were produced in Britain. However, as soldiers found the hooked quillon of this bayonet to be a nuisance, the decision was made to abandon the hook design in 1913 before it had even been used in earnest. The United States of America's Model 1917 was a copy of

the British 1914 Pattern bayonet design, itself a modification of the 1907 Pattern but with a longer, straight cross guard.

Another inconvenience of a long bayonet is its weight. Some countries tried to retain the length of the sword bayonet while also avoiding the weight problem. The French developed the long epee bayonet for their 1886 Pattern Lebel rifle, the very narrow blade of which was given a cruciform cross-section to reduce weight even further while at the same time retaining strength. The Russians – perhaps the most poorly equipped major army of the war – went one step further and removed even more weight by abandoning a conventional hilt and using a socket bayonet with a cruciform-sectioned blade on the 1891 Moisin Nagant 7.62mm rifle. This in itself was simply a continuation of tradition, an almost identical form of bayonet being used on the Russian Model 1871 Berdan rifle. In Britain, the contemporary long Model 1895 socket bayonet was designed for the new Lee-Enfield rifle.

BELOW An early British 1907 Pattern complete with hooked quillon. Although the hook was officially declared obsolete in 1913, some still entered World War I in their unmodified state.

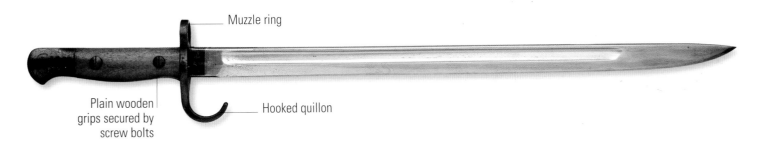

Muzzle ring

Plain wooden grips secured by screw bolts

Hooked quillon

Grooved metal handle

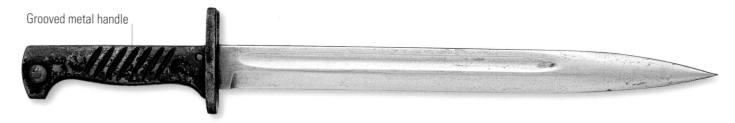

World War I German bayonet forms

Germany had adopted a short "knife" bayonet for the Model 1884 Mauser rifle, and this bayonet continued in use on the Mauser Gewehr Model 1898. The Germans therefore entered the war with a shorter bayonet than those of most of the other protagonists. Even so, the *seitengewehr* (sidearm) bayonet originally designed for the Gewehr 1898 rifle had a blade that was even longer than that of the British 1907 Pattern, and it also saw service. In 1905, Germany found a middle ground in bayonet design with the introduction of the so-called "butcher knife" or "butcher blade" bayonet. The terminology was probably invented by the Allies as part of a propaganda campaign, but the blade certainly had an unusual

shape with its increasing width towards the point, reminiscent of the British Elcho of 1871. In various forms this new German bayonet was probably the most widely used during the war. By 1916 Germany was suffering from an increasingly stressed economy and a shortage of raw materials as a result of an Allied naval blockade. In an effort to keep its troops supplied, Germany developed simplified designs and manufacturing techniques. Even old sword blades were cut down and fitted with mounts for Mauser rifles. The Germans also began to recycle captured weapons, and many Belgian, French and Russian bayonets were converted to fit German rifles. These two types of weapon were generally referred to as *ersatz*, or "emergency", bayonets and exist in huge variety.

Bayonets of World War II

After World War I, the relevance of the bayonet in modern warfare was frequently questioned. The number of bayonet wounds inflicted in World War I appears to have been minimal. For example, one study showed that of a sample of 200,000 wounds suffered by British soldiers, only 600 were caused by bayonets, while the American forces estimated that only .024 per cent of their injuries were bayonet-related. Even so, bayonets remained a standard part of the infantryman's equipment on both sides during World War II. Some of the types common in World War I remained in use during World War II, the Japanese Arisaka bayonet being one example. But the general trend was towards shorter versions.

The British began to replace their 1907 Pattern with a series of short knife bayonets. Some, like the No 5 bayonet for the Jungle Carbine, had a more or less conventional hilt similar to that of the 1907 Pattern.

LEFT British troops, equipped with standard-issue bayonets fitted to their rifles, make fun of Mussolini's characteristic arrogant posture in this portrait of *Il Duce* after the capture of Cyrenaica, Libya, in 1941.

RIGHT Propaganda posters such as this American example invariably show idealized soldiers dramatically wielding rifles with fixed bayonets. The bayonet was synonymous with the tough, indomitable "good guy".

Its blade was very different, not only in being much shorter but also in being more akin to that of the fabled Bowie knife. But most of this new series utilized what was in effect a return to the principle of the socket bayonet. The No 4 bayonet for the new No 4 rifle had a cruciform-section blade very similar to that of the French 1886 Lebel but only 20cm (9in) in length. It was fitted to a relatively simple block with a locking device for attachment to the muzzle of the rifle. The rifle muzzle itself had two lugs which engaged with internal slots in the "socket" or muzzle ring of the bayonet. This more or less experimental Mk I bayonet was quickly replaced in 1940 by the Mk II, which had a plain round "spike" or "pig-sticker" blade and was easier and cheaper to manufacture.

This trend continued with the No 7 bayonet. This again had the Bowie-type blade and a complex hilt, which allowed it in one mode to be gripped and used as a knife. The pommel could also be swivelled through 180 degrees, allowing it to act as a socket for fitting to the rifle. Both the No 5 and No 7 bayonets are also characterized by their very large muzzle rings. In the case of the No 5, this allowed the bayonet to accommodate the mouth of the flash hider (the device that masked the firing flash). In the case of the No 7, the "muzzle ring" did not function in that capacity at all. Finally, the No 9 bayonet was produced for the Royal Navy and was a cross between the No 5 and No 4 series in that it had a Bowie blade fitted to a socket.

When the United States entered the war in 1941, most American infantrymen were armed with the pre-World War I 41cm (16in) M1905 Pattern bayonet (later renamed the M1942). But like most other nations, the United States soon recognized the necessity of utilizing a shorter knife pattern, which could also be used as a fighting knife. The M1 bayonet, which had a much shorter 25cm (10in) blade, was introduced in 1943.

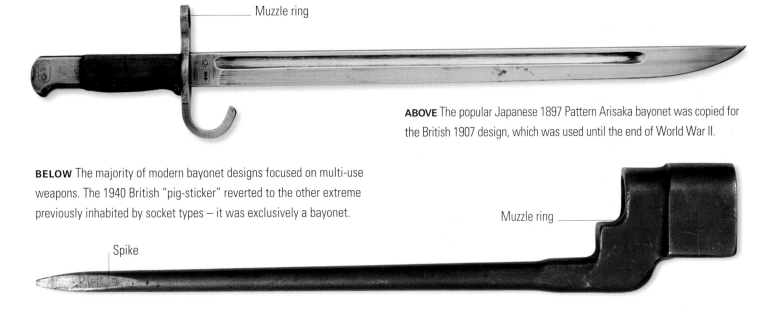

Muzzle ring

ABOVE The popular Japanese 1897 Pattern Arisaka bayonet was copied for the British 1907 design, which was used until the end of World War II.

BELOW The majority of modern bayonet designs focused on multi-use weapons. The 1940 British "pig-sticker" reverted to the other extreme previously inhabited by socket types – it was exclusively a bayonet.

Spike

Muzzle ring

The bayonet in conflict

The effectiveness of the bayonet not only as a hand-to-hand combat weapon but as a psychological weapon was clearly demonstrated during the Battle of the Reichswald Forest in February 1945. At one stage, groups of British and German soldiers were engaged in a bitter firefight as they hid in ditches and holes. With no more than 200m (650ft) between them, the British decided to rush the German line. They fixed bayonets and ran forward. As soon as the British charge began, the Germans ceased fire and raised their hands in surrender. For these modern soldiers, trained to kill from afar and demoralized by many months of continual combat, the threat of "cold steel" was clearly too much. This was the last bayonet charge of the war.

The fighting knives of World Wars I and II

Above all, World War I was characterized by trench warfare. After an initial advance into Belgium and northern France, the German army was halted by the Allied forces. Both sides "dug in" and fortified their positions with trench systems that extended for hundreds of miles. This stalemate situation led to hand-to-hand fighting on a limited scale. If one side mounted a full-scale assault, rushing en masse across the landmines and barbed wire of "no man's land", any troops who were fortunate enough to get past the enemy machine guns had to be prepared to fight at close quarters in the confined environment of the enemy trench. Here the long-bladed bayonet was of little use, since there was no space to wield it. Trench combat thus necessitated the military reinstatement of the dagger, or fighting knife.

Some early trench knives were simply fashioned from cut-down bayonets, although they were also made from many other objects, including the metal posts that were used to support the barbed-wire

ABOVE Bayonets line the trenches along the Western Front where German soldiers keep guard during World War I.

defences. As well as their role as close-range combat weapons, trench knives were also useful to small raiding parties sent into enemy territory to take prisoners or gather intelligence, when the ability to kill silently was all-important.

World War I brought the fighting knife officially back to the battlefield after a 200-year absence. Its modern relevance having been acknowledged, the development of the military fighting knife continued throughout the period between the wars.

The Mark I trench knife

During the last five months of World War I, the United States made an extensive study of all the diverse forms of trench knife then in use. It rated them on several points, including the blade's weight, length and shape, suitability to be carried while crawling and the probability of the knife being knocked from the hand. The results of these tests led to the development of the Mark I trench knife, which was intended to combine all of the best aspects of the weapons included in the study. The Mark I was composed of a 17cm (7in)

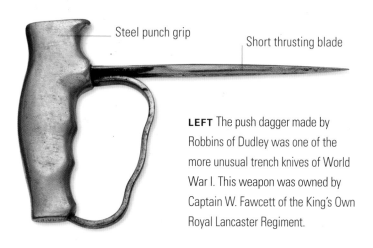

Steel punch grip

Short thrusting blade

LEFT The push dagger made by Robbins of Dudley was one of the more unusual trench knives of World War I. This weapon was owned by Captain W. Fawcett of the King's Own Royal Lancaster Regiment.

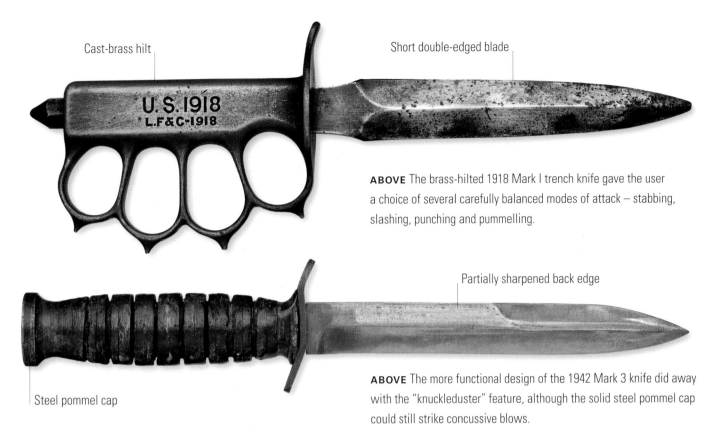

Cast-brass hilt

Short double-edged blade

ABOVE The brass-hilted 1918 Mark I trench knife gave the user a choice of several carefully balanced modes of attack – stabbing, slashing, punching and pummelling.

Partially sharpened back edge

Steel pommel cap

ABOVE The more functional design of the 1942 Mark 3 knife did away with the "knuckleduster" feature, although the solid steel pommel cap could still strike concussive blows.

double-edged blade designed for both cutting and thrusting, and a cast-bronze hilt that incorporated individual loops for the fingers, forming a knuckleduster. It even had a pointed nut on the pommel to secure the hilt and blade together, but which was also able to fracture the skull if used with sufficient force. Although none were manufactured after the 120,000 produced in the United States and France in 1918, this weapon remained in use alongside later knives until it was declared obsolete in January 1945.

The Mark 3 trench knife

When the United States entered the war in 1941, the only fighting knife in the US Army's inventory was the Mark I. A new production run of this model was proposed but then ruled out; the bronze required for the cast hilt was a critical strategic metal, and it was felt that a better design could be found. After several studies, the new knife was designated Mark 3, and was described in the US Army's Catalog of Standard Ordnance Items as "developed to fill the need in modern warfare for hand-to-hand fighting … designed for such shock units as parachute troops and rangers." The knife had a short, straight blade 17cm (7in) long, with a 7cm (3in) "false" edge, and a corrugated grip constructed of compressed leather washers. Some 590,247 Mark 3s were manufactured before production was cancelled in August 1942.

CACCIALI VIA!

SOTTOSCRIVETE AL PRESTITO

ABOVE A typical patriotic poster of World War I, this one Italian, showing a brave soldier defending his home and loved ones.

Cross-hatched grip

Flattened diamond-section blade

The FS "commando" knife

In 1940 the British Army formed its first Special Forces unit, the "Commandos", to strike key targets along the Normandy coast of France. The training of this small, elite force was entrusted to Captain William Fairbairn and Captain Eric Sykes. Both had been members of the Shanghai police force, where they had studied martial arts and learned their special skills of armed and unarmed combat, including the ability to use anything at hand, however unlikely, as an effective weapon. They also learnt how to kill silently.

When they took up their new duties, Fairbairn and Sykes discovered the Commandos were armed with a

ABOVE A Fairbairn-Sykes "commando" knife, c.1942. The design of the weapon is remarkably medieval, with a long grip, short cross guard, and diamond-section cut-and-thrust blade.

knuckleduster-type knife, the BC41. But Fairbairn and Sykes had their own views on knives and approached the Wilkinson Sword Company, Britain's best-known manufacturer of edged weapons, with an original design. The first shipment of Fairbairn-Sykes (FS) fighting knives arrived in January 1941. The FS knife had a tapering 18cm (7in) double-edged blade, a simple oval cross guard, and a long, slightly bulbous, metal handle. The first pattern of knives had fine cross-hatching to provide a firm grip when the hands were wet, whether with rainwater, seawater or blood. Later models had grips encircled by a series of ribs or grooves. The blades were honed to an edge that would cut paper, and the cross guard was not to prevent an opponent's knife sliding down the blade but to prevent the user's hand from doing the same and suffering serious injury when thrusting with the knife. The knife was made so that the point of balance was on the hilt just behind the cross guard.

The preferred method of carrying the knife was in a sheath sewn to the inside of the left trouser pocket – a pistol was to be carried in the right-hand pocket. But the knife could be worn in many places – on the belt, down the boot or up the sleeve. It could also be sewn to the uniform in any other way that the individual soldier preferred. Many versions of the FS knife were produced, and its design was copied by the Special Forces of other countries; 3,420 were delivered to the US Army in 1943, this version being designated V-42. More British-made FS knives were sold to American soldiers stationed in England before they were deployed to continental Europe or North Africa. The US Marine Corps also adopted the knife for a short period.

LEFT The Fairbairn-Sykes knife could be worn in many different ways. This photograph of a British Commando involved in the raid on Dieppe, taken on 20 August 1942, shows one strapped to the ankle.

The US Navy Mark 2 and the USMC "KA-BAR"

During World War II, the US Navy developed its own fighting knives, primarily for shore personnel near the front line and combat swimmers, or "frogmen". The US Navy Mark 2 Utility Knife was a relation of the Army Mark 3; like it, the Navy Mark 2 had a handle composed of compressed leather washers. The blade was more like that of a small Bowie knife, being nearly 18cm (7in) long with a clipped point. The first combat knife made specifically for the US Marine Corps was identical to the Navy Mark 2 apart from the marks on the blade. Officially called the "fighting-utility knife", it soon became known among Marines as the "KA-BAR", after the trademark of the Union Cutlery Company, which manufactured the earliest versions. By 1943 these knives were in general use, and they remained the US Marine's trusted companion in many subsequent campaigns.

20th-century ceremonial knives

Swords, in both past civilian life and within military forces up to the present day, have been the primary symbol of rank and still have their place on the parade ground and at other ceremonial occasions. In some instances, knives of one form or another have also served a similar function.

The naval dirk worn by the midshipman originally marked him out as a junior officer, and awards of this classic weapon have continued to be made. Similarly, the elaborately adorned dirk of the Scots Guards once served them on the field of conflict and now serves them on parade. The dirk is not only an ongoing part of a military tradition, but also an important part of Highland dress and is still seen on "civilian" occasions such as weddings and other celebrations. The unusual but famous traditional kukri was often worn as part of

BELOW Along with the Fairbairn-Sykes commando knife, the US Navy Mark 2, perhaps most famous as the US Marine Corps' KA-BAR, is one of the world's most successful modern combat knives.

ABOVE A Boy Scout in uniform with an unusual sheath knife, with wooden slab grips instead of grips of imitation stag or compressed leather washers.

ceremonial dress by the British Army's Gurkha regiment. The sight of these knives in those same hands created a legendary and formidable combination, sufficient to instil fear in the heart of anyone who might face them in battle.

On a completely different level, the traditional parade uniform of the Boy Scouts' would have been incomplete at one time without the sheath knife. It wasn't, of course, carried as a weapon but as a tool for use in field craft.

Compressed leather grip

Clipped point

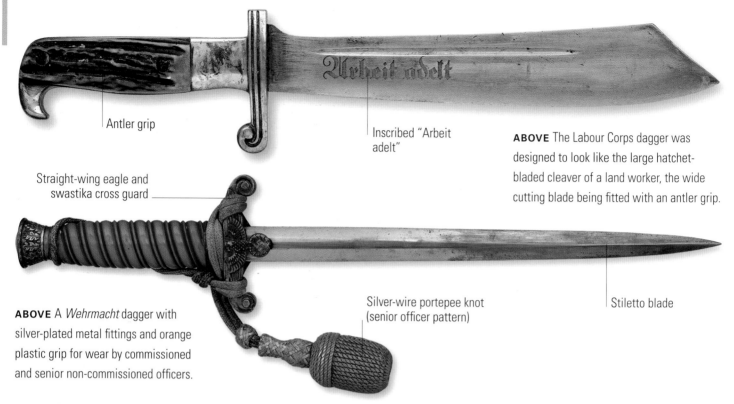

Antler grip

Inscribed "Arbeit adelt"

ABOVE The Labour Corps dagger was designed to look like the large hatchet-bladed cleaver of a land worker, the wide cutting blade being fitted with an antler grip.

Straight-wing eagle and swastika cross guard

ABOVE A *Wehrmacht* dagger with silver-plated metal fittings and orange plastic grip for wear by commissioned and senior non-commissioned officers.

Silver-wire portepee knot (senior officer pattern)

Stiletto blade

Daggers of the Third Reich

The concept of the "dress" dagger flourished during the German Third Reich, and an almost boundless variety were created for every branch of the military, quasi-military and even many non-military state organizations. In 1933 a delegation from the sword-making city of Solingen approached Germany's new leader Adolf Hitler with a proposal. It was suggested that the Nazi Party adopt various types of sword and dagger as status and distinguishing symbols for its members. Solingen had been a world-famous centre for the production of fine-edged weapons since the Middle Ages, but defeat in World War I had hit its industry very badly and many of its craftsmen were out of work. Hitler and some of his close associates had embraced and almost resurrected certain aspects of German medieval culture as part of Nazi ideology, and they enthusiastically approved the idea.

The first member of what would become the huge family of Nazi daggers was introduced in 1934 for the *Sturm Abteilung* ("Stormtroopers"), or SA, the Nazi Party's private police force. Solingen craftsmen took as their model the characteristically Germanic "Swiss" or "Holbein" dagger of the 16th century. The design was simplified but the overall form of the I-shaped hilt, with brown grips made of walnut or similar wood, remained unchanged. The broad, spear-pointed blade was etched with the motto *Alles für Deutschland* ("Everything for Germany"). Shortly thereafter, a very

BELOW An off-duty German officer in Paris in 1941, his uniform complete with standard dress dagger.

RIGHT This 1937 photo taken in Nuremberg of Josef Goebbels (left) and Hermann Göring, two of Hitler's closest aides, shows Göring with one of the many forms of Nazi "Holbein"-type dress dagger.

similar dagger was commissioned for the *Schutzstaffel* ("Protective Squadron"), or SS, the Nazis' elite guard. This weapon was almost identical to the SA version, apart from its black hilt and the motto on the blade: *Meine Ehre heißt Treue* ("My Honour is Named Loyalty"). The Army, Airforce and Navy each had their own distinctive daggers, the most distinctive of all, perhaps, being the 1st Pattern *Luftwaffe* ("Airforce") dagger produced in classical "Holbein" style and with a large circular pommel and winged cross guard.

Gradually, nearly every organization of the Nazi Party acquired its own ceremonial knife. They included the Motor Transport Corps, the National Political Education Institute and the Hitler *Jugend* ("Hitler Youth"), an equivalent of the Boy Scout movement but with its main focus on training young minds in Nazi ideology. Dress daggers were also produced for the Postal Protection Service, Waterways Protection Police, Diplomatic Service, the Red Cross and National Forestry Service. Even the Fire Service had parade axes for firemen and daggers for officers.

One of the most distinctive civil service daggers was awarded to the *Reicharbeitsdienst* ("Labour Corps"). Designed to look suitably rustic, the workman-like Labour Corps dagger, often referred to as a "hewer", had a broad chopping blade, staghorn grip and appropriate motto: *Arbeit adelt* ("Labour ennobles"). Special versions of many daggers were also produced for officers and for presentation purposes.

Perhaps one of the rarest presentation daggers is the naval dress dagger awarded by Grand Admiral Erich Raeder, of which only six are thought to exist. It has an elaborately decorated scabbard, a Damascus blade and a 17-diamond swastika in the pommel.

This almost obsessive trend in dagger design by the Third Reich was never copied by other countries. However, many of them adopted ceremonial daggers on a far more limited scale. Until the 1950s, Soviet Russia and many countries under Soviet influence issued such daggers to their army, air force and naval officers. Some South American countries also used them. The Japanese also adopted dress daggers within their military circles. But on the whole this trend has now largely disappeared, and these daggers are preserved only by collectors.

BELOW The SA dagger, manufactured between 1934 and 1945, was perhaps the most common of the many Nazi daggers of "Holbein" form.

SA badge rondel

Inscribed "Alles für Deutschland"

Nazi eagle insignia

African knives and daggers

As is true of tribal cultures everywhere in the world, the common traditional weapons in Africa were the bow and arrow and the spear. But the native peoples of the African continent also created a profusion of other weapons, including a bewildering multitude of daggers and knives. Despite a generally simple level of technology, the work of African bladesmiths is exceptional in terms of its quality, originality, functionality and design.

Although copper and bronze were commonly worked throughout Africa, iron had been the predominant metal for making weapons since ancient times. Iron ore is found in most parts of Africa – mined but also found close to the surface near rivers or deposited in dry river beds. By the 4th or 3rd century BC, iron was being worked in what is now northwestern Tanzania, northern Nigeria and the Sudan. Excavations of the ancient Nubian city of Meroe, on the east bank of the Nile, north of Khartoum, revealed, along with over 200 pyramids, gigantic slag

heaps which testify to very considerable ironworking activities. The context of the excavation site demonstrates that iron was being worked there on an industrial scale by at least the 1st century AD.

In theory, the design of an African edged weapon should be characteristic of, or relate to the specific tribe that created it. However, a well-made weapon was always valuable, a useful trade item or literal form of currency, and so it should not be surprising that the weapons forged by a particular tribe were found in the possession of many of their neighbours. Migration and displacement due to environmental or territorial factors also disseminated distinctive weapons forms over much larger areas.

It is very difficult, therefore, to date particular African weapons precisely or to identify their exact place of origin positively. Weapons studied by early explorers from Europe were usually named after the area where they were found. But this may not have been the land of the tribe who made them. Also, tribal names could be derived from many different things, features in the landscape for example, and one tribe might have more than one name. Yet it is possible to discuss in a general way the areas or cultures that are most closely associated with distinctive knife forms.

Baule knives and daggers

The Baule tribe of the Ivory Coast are famous not only for their wooden figurines and masks but also for their skill in working iron, brass, bronze and gold, and the Baule smith was a skilled weapons maker. The blades of Baule knives and daggers vary considerably in form. Some are long and very wide, being either steeply

LEFT Knives and other edged weapons were collected in Africa by many 19th-century travellers. In this illustration a group of objects collected by Professor Friedrich Ratzel in the Upper Congo, 1898, is shown. The group appears largely to be made up of Ngala, Ngombe and Kuba weapons.

ABOVE This rare 19th-century drawing shows the traditional metalworking processes practised in Africa for hundreds of years, including smelting iron ore in a bloomery and beating a lump of iron, or "bloom".

tapered down the top half or tightly waisted and leaf-shaped. Others are shorter, having a simple, straight shape with a clipped point, not unlike a Japanese dagger or tanto. Another Baule knife form, specifically for ceremonial or ritual purposes, is very wide, curved and sickle-like. Hilts are usually carved of wood, while scabbards are often made of leather exquisitely tooled with geometric patterns or covered with brightly coloured shells.

The knives and daggers of the Azande tribe

Perhaps one of the most martial of all African tribes, the Azande inhabited parts of what is now the Democratic Republic of Congo, southwestern Sudan, and the southeastern end of the Central African Republic. Although technically very militant by traditional standards, the Azande took careful measures to prevent excessive violence in war, which for them was to a great extent symbolic. A battle could be decided by the death or even wounding of an individual opponent, while surrounded and trapped enemies would be allowed to escape, their symbolic defeat having been achieved.

The knives and daggers of the Azande are well made and finely decorated. Ceremonial weapons sometimes have blades of copper, while most practical examples

are of iron. Their long leaf blades are designed both for cutting and thrusting, and are generally decorated with tight groups of file-lines or grooves. Sometimes the blades are pierced with large holes or slots. The hilts are often covered with narrow ribbons of copper or bronze, which are either wrapped or plaited around them. Especially valuable knives are sometimes fitted with hilts of elephant ivory, carved with geometric designs.

The Azande traditionally used knives as a form of currency. An Azande dowry, or bridewealth, for example, might be given in the form of a number (usually 40) of dagger blades.

ABOVE Knives and other edged weapons often have purposes other than combat. These elaborate Congolese throwing knives, made of copper, are intended as tributes for Azande leaders from their vassals.

Knives and daggers of the Fang tribe

Living in southern Cameroon, the Gabonese Republic and Equatorial Guinea, the Fang are the creators not only of the remarkable *bieri*, reliquary sculptures that probably had a strong influence on the early development of cubism, but also of the so-called "bird's-head" knife. The concept of this strange, other-worldly weapon may have been inspired by the African horn raven (*Bucorvus caver*). The bird's-head knife is often thought to be a throwing knife, although this is debatable.

The Fang are also known for a long dagger, which is somewhat reminiscent of the Roman gladius, or short sword, having a straight, wide blade. These practical fighting daggers were combined, like the gladius, with a large, square shield, which protected most of the warrior's body while he closed with his enemy and stabbed him with the knife.

ABOVE The Fang *bieri* or "bird's-head" knife is one of the most striking of all African weapons. The triangular blade cut-out contrasts with its gentle curves, a quality that appealed to Cubist artists, such as Picasso.

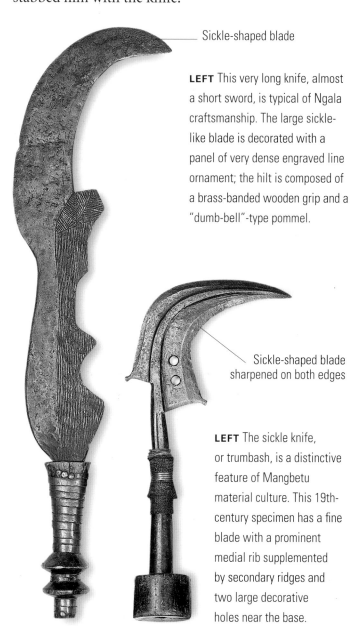

Sickle-shaped blade

LEFT This very long knife, almost a short sword, is typical of Ngala craftsmanship. The large sickle-like blade is decorated with a panel of very dense engraved line ornament; the hilt is composed of a brass-banded wooden grip and a "dumb-bell"-type pommel.

Sickle-shaped blade sharpened on both edges

LEFT The sickle knife, or trumbash, is a distinctive feature of Mangbetu material culture. This 19th-century specimen has a fine blade with a prominent medial rib supplemented by secondary ridges and two large decorative holes near the base.

The Mangbetu hooked sickle knife

The trumbash, of the Mangbetu in the northwestern corner of the Democratic Republic of Congo is a hooked sickle knife, and easily recognized. The wide blade is formed with a graceful if abrupt right-angle change about halfway along its length. The edges of the blade trace various paths in relation to the centre line, some examples being more angular while others are more rounded and uniformly curved.

Whatever the exact shape, these weapons always possess a singular boldness. The blades are usually ridged in all sorts of highly individual ways, with some ridges being very sharp and narrow, others being wider and flat-topped. Some blades are pierced with pairs of large, round holes, and are sometimes forged with short, knob-like projections at the base of both edges. All of these aspects contribute to a sense of the Mangbetu sickle knife being a piece of abstract art as well as a weapon. The handle is usually carved out of wood or ivory. Many have pommels in the form of a

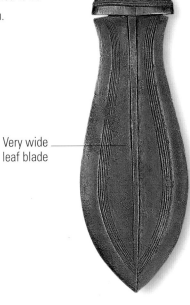

RIGHT The form of the Kuba ikul attests to this object's role as a peaceful ceremonial object. It is beautifully made and pleasing to the eye, with fluid, flowing lines, but it has been purposely designed to be inconvenient as a weapon.

Very wide leaf blade

LEFT This intricately decorated Kuba mask displays the rich artistic culture of this Central African people. The weapons they produce are equally ornate and complex in their design.

large, cylindrical block, sometimes studded with brass nails. The heavy pommel of the trumbash even led to a nonsensical myth that they were dropped on the heads of enemies by warriors hiding in trees. Other grips are carved in the form of a human head and upper body. These, like many Mangbetu figures, are immediately identifiable because of the elongated skulls that they depict; traditionally, Mangbetu babies' heads were bound to induce them to grow into a stretched form that was considered to be eminently attractive.

Knives and daggers of the Kuba

The Kuba kingdom, a pre-colonial state centred near the land south of the Kasai River in Central Africa, was actually a conglomeration of many smaller tribes conquered by the original Kuba or Buschoog ("people of the throwing knife"). Famous as artists obsessed with glorious surface ornament, the Kuba produced extraordinary helmet-like masks, richly patterned textiles and beautiful weapons, the most idiosyncratic of which is the ikul. This very wide, leaf-bladed knife is said to have been introduced by King Shyaam aMbul aNgoong, the founder of the Kuba kingdom, in around 1600. The ikul was an emblem of peace. It is often

depicted on Kuba king figures, or *ndop*, which portray the monarch with an ikul in his left hand and an ilwoon, or sword of war, in his right, symbolizing the ruler's dual role as war-leader and peacemaker.

Ikuls are made with blades of iron or copper fitted with grips of wood, often inlaid with brass or copper; to further accentuate their role as symbols of peace, some ikuls are made entirely of carved wood.

Knives of the Ngala and the Ndjembo people

Congolese Ngala knives appear in three main forms. The first is very long, double-edged and curved in a shallow, graceful arc. The second is shorter and wider, the blade often tear-shaped with one or two ridges. The third is almost a form of machete – wide-bladed and long, decorated with ridges, profuse file-lines and cross-hatching. The leading edge is recurved and the trailing edge cut into a series of cuspings, the point forming a stout hook. These knives were often taken to be decapitation implements, but are more likely to have had ceremonial significance. Closely related to the Ngala knife is that of the neighbouring Ndjembo. This is of a similar length but straight until it divides into two long points that curve inwards in a crescent shape.

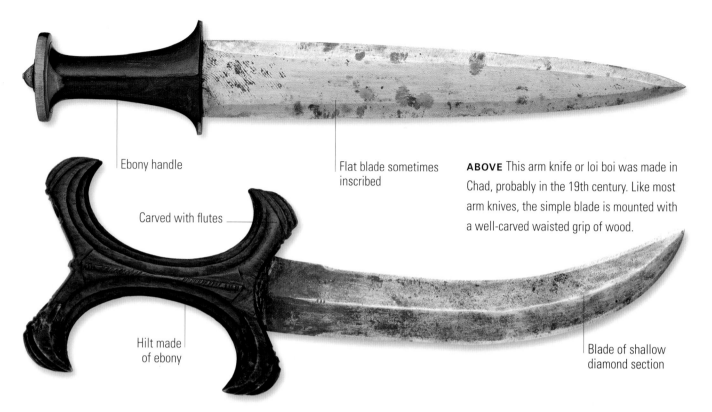

Ebony handle

Flat blade sometimes inscribed

ABOVE This arm knife or loi boi was made in Chad, probably in the 19th century. Like most arm knives, the simple blade is mounted with a well-carved waisted grip of wood.

Carved with flutes

Hilt made of ebony

Blade of shallow diamond section

African arm daggers

The dagger worn on the arm, or loi boi, is a uniquely African weapon popular among various tribes in many different regions of the continent. Generally it is worn in a scabbard attached by means of leather loops or thongs to the inner side of the left forearm, with the blade pointing up towards the elbow and the handle sitting close to the inside of the wrist. From here the arm dagger can be swiftly drawn when needed. Occasionally, it is instead worn on the outside of the upper arm with the blade facing downwards.

Arm daggers are associated with a number of the peoples inhabiting the Sahara and the Sahel – the border country of the Sudan between the northern desert regions and the central tropics. Northern examples are very often fitted with European knife or bayonet blades, or cut-down sword blades.

In northwest Africa the tribe most famous for their use of the arm dagger, or telek, is the Tuareg. Tribes in northern Nigeria, particularly the Nube and the Berom, also make arm daggers in the Tuareg style.

Arm daggers are also very popular among the Hausa of Cameroon. As in most traditional societies, a high-quality dagger for the Hausa reflects the owner's wealth and social status. Hausa daggers are not unlike Swiss daggers of the 15th and 16th centuries – with vaguely I-shaped hilts and wide, straight-sided blades that taper rapidly down the last third of their length to a very sharp stabbing point.

ABOVE This Sudanese dagger, which was made around 1900, has a less common curved blade and displays an ergonomic hilt not unlike the European baselard or Indian chilanum.

BELOW The Tuareg warriors of northwest Africa carry a variety of weapons but their most distinctive side arm is the telek or arm dagger.

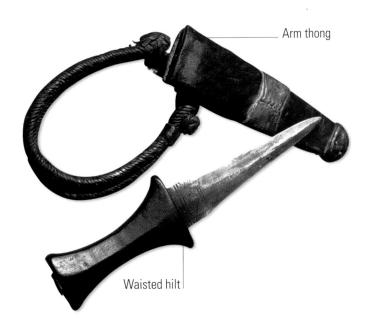

Arm thong

Waisted hilt

ABOVE The arm dagger is a common traditional weapon in many parts of North Africa. This Sudanese example is reasonably typical, with a simple waisted hilt and arm-thonged scabbard.

African throwing knives

The vast group of African multi-bladed weapons that ethnographers have commonly awarded the term "throwing knives" are unlike any other weapons found anywhere else in the world. Many types do not in fact appear to have been intended for throwing, while others, like the Fang "bird's-head" knife, could be thrown on occasion, though this was probably not its main method of use.

However, some types are without question carefully engineered as lethal aerial blades, which spin through the air like multi-bladed, razor-sharp boomerangs. Indeed, the earliest versions of these unusual weapons

may have developed from the very ancient idea of the throwing stick. Emil Torday, an early 20th-century traveller, collector and museum curator, wrote poetically about the use of throwing knives by Kuba warriors:

… then all of a sudden, some objects, glittering in the sun as if they were thunderbolts, come whirling with a weird hum through the air. The enemy warriors raise their shields; the shining mystery strikes it, rebounds into the air and continues to the attack; it smites the warrior behind his defence with its cruel blades. A weapon which is capable of killing behind a shield cannot fail to cause a panic …

African throwing knives are usually classified into two very general groups: the circular type and the F-type. The former have blades that extend away from the centre of gravity, usually in three directions, while the latter are, to a greater or lesser degree, shaped in the form of the letter "F".

In addition to the Kuba, a great many tribes claim throwing knives as their traditional weapons, including the Azande, Ingessana (Tabi Hills, Sudan), Hutu (Rwanda, Burundi), Bwaka (Central African Republic), Ngbaka (northwest Congo), Masalit (Darfur, Sudan), Sara (Chad) and Nsakara (northeast Congo). The throwing knives of this last tribe are said to be some of the best, with their centre of gravity perfectly placed to produce a good spin. The flight characteristics of Nsakara throwing knives are considered excellent, the slight angling of the blade relative to its plane converting rotational motion into lift, essentially creating a somewhat stable propeller effect which increases the weapon's range and accuracy.

BELOW This Somali throwing knife appears to have been used a number of times, whether it was intended for fighting or not. Three of the blades appear to have been broken off and welded back in place.

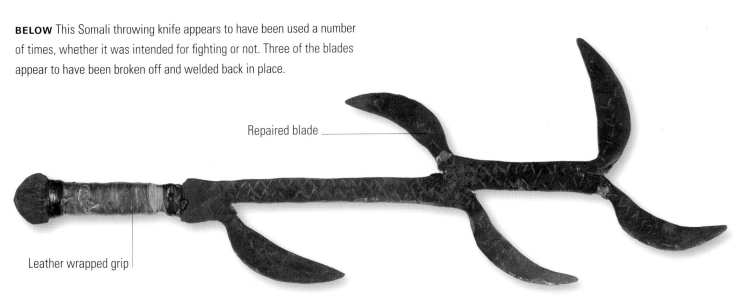

Repaired blade

Leather wrapped grip

Persian and Middle Eastern daggers

Persian daggers from before the 15th century are difficult to identify, as very few of them remain. But from the mid-1400s onwards, a greater number of spectacular pieces have survived. The best 15th-, 16th- and 17th-century examples are signed or have key features that allow them to be more accurately dated and attributed. Some embody distinctive Persian styles, while others represent general fashions throughout the Middle East.

Fine gold damascening

Hilt of rock-crystal

ABOVE An extremely fine Persian dagger from the 17th century mounted with an expensive white jade hilt inlaid with gold.

ABOVE The hilt of this dagger, like the example above, was made in the 1600s in Persia. It is carved from a single piece of almost flawless rock-crystal, a rare material requiring very skilled carving.

For centuries Persia was at the heart of the Islamic world, situated between Turkey and Arabia to the west and Muslim Afghanistan and India to the east. It was a geographical, cultural and military crossroads. The Seljuk Turks ruled Persia from 1037 until the early 13th century, when they lost it to the Khwarezmids, another Turkic people of Mamluk origin. The Shahs of the Khwarezmid Empire in turn had to defend Persia against Genghis Khan, who in 1219 seized key locations along the Silk Road including Samarkand (in modern Uzbekistan) and Otar (a city in what is today Kazakhstan). Subsequently most of Persia became a part of the vast Mongol Empire. Not until 1292 did it return to Muslim rule with the conversion of Ghazan Khan (1271–1304) Persia's Mongol overlord.

Years of conquest and reconquest followed Ghazan's secession from the Chino-Mongol Empire, the borders being continually redrawn by successive invaders, most notably the Turco-Mongol warlord Timur the Lame (1336–1405), who conquered Persia and established the Muslim Timurid Dynasty at the end of the 14th century. The Timurid Emirs ruled Persia for nearly 100 years until the establishment of the Safavid Dynasty in 1500. Under the Safavids, Persia entered its greatest cultural period since the first Islamic conquest in the 7th century.

Weapons production in Persia

Persian weapons were famous throughout the Middle East from ancient times. Samarkand and Isfahan were especially renowned as centres for the production of the finest swords and daggers. Persia was wealthy in the natural resources required for the production of high-quality weapons – iron, silver and gold. A long tradition of the scientific study of metals in the Islamic world led to the development of "watered" steel, fusions of high- and medium-carbon steels that displayed in good measure the two key properties of an excellent blade – hardness and elasticity. The extraordinary silk-like patterns that formed on the surfaces of these blades when etched with acid were a sure sign of their quality.

The problems of identification

Today it is often very difficult to identify daggers, and blades in general, as specifically Persian, partly because so few have survived from earlier times, but mainly because the arms trade operated on a scale far larger and more expansive than Persia itself. Indian blades were imported into Persia, where they might be decorated and assembled into complete weapons by the local craftsmen, while Persian work was also exported, not only back to India but also west into Arabia and Turkey.

Our modern understanding is further hampered by the fact that specialist researchers did not begin the scholarly study of Persian weapons dating from the 15th to 19th centuries until the 1970s. Thus a great deal of basic research is still lacking, and ways of dating daggers in particular, though now much improved, are still very generalized. Indeed, many daggers that bear dated inscriptions remained unread until the late 20th century.

ABOVE Daggers have been made throughout the Islamic world for hundreds of years. This scene of a Yemeni daggersmith's workshop is undoubtedly a sight that has remained largely unchanged in centuries.

The kylin clue

Depictions of the mythical beasts known as kylins appear in art throughout the Middle and Far East. Although exact portrayals vary, the kylin is usually shown as a hooved, dragon-like creature with a scaly body and antlers similar to those of a stag. It is often depicted with its body bathed in fire. It is invariably believed to be a creature sent to punish the sinful, or to protect the good from evil. It is also sometimes considered the pet of divine beings.

Kylins appear on certain early Persian daggers of the 15th century. The specific nature of these appearances, along with dragons and birds, is closely comparable to the decoration on the exquisite leather bindings on Persian manuscripts of the 1400s. Although precise dating of manuscripts of this period is difficult, there seems to be no suggestion that any of them could be later than 1500. It seems likely, therefore, that the presence of such beasts on the hilt of a fine Persian dagger is a good indicator of an early date.

RIGHT The kylin is as iconic in Eastern culture as dragons are in Western medieval and Renaissance art. The horned heads, scales and fiery tails of these Chinese figures are very similar to dragons.

LEFT Some Persian daggers are covered in extraordinary multicoloured decoration. This one includes a hilt mounted with cabochons, highly polished rubies and a scabbard ornamented with gold and enamel.

Dating Persian daggers

Although curved blades have been traditionally preferred throughout the Middle East, many of the best Persian daggers carry straight double-edged blades. Fine Persian blades of the 15th, 16th and 17th centuries are usually decorated with poetic inscriptions. The weapons can be dated through careful examination of the language and type of script used in the inscriptions. Verses in Turkic might lead one to assume that a particular dagger was of Turkish origin. But Turkic was also used by the Safavid Court. In such cases the script itself, rather than the language, might be the most vital clue. Turkic verses sometimes appear on daggers written in fluid *nasta 'liq* script, a style of writing that originated in Persia.

Another important indicator of the date of a fine Persian dagger is the exact character of the background against which the script is set. For example, 15th-century blades tend to have inscriptions set against a plain background, while in the 16th and 17th centuries the backgrounds were usually filled in with flowers, leaves and coiling vines, the density of which seems to increase along with the date of the work.

LEFT Some Persian daggers are covered in extraordinary multicoloured decoration. This one includes a hilt mounted with cabochons, highly polished rubies and a scabbard ornamented with gold and enamel.

Decoration and inscriptions

The best daggers produced in Persia and Turkey were usually fitted with hilts carved out of rock-crystal, jade or ivory, or forged of watered steel. Expensive dagger hilts and scabbards were also studded with gems, cabochons often being preferred, perhaps because they resembled drops of blood or water. One poem found on several surviving daggers, in Persian *ruba'i* rhyme, includes a vivid reference to this form of decoration:

> *Every time that thy dagger talked of vengeance,*
> *It brought the times into confusion by its shedding*
> *   of blood!*
> *By the elegance and purity of the stones which are on it,*
> *It recalled a willow-leaf covered with dew!*

Persian blade inscriptions were usually evocative of, or at least appropriate to the function or character of the dagger, both as a weapon and as a symbol:

> *I wanted so much to have a gleaming dagger,*
> *That each of my ribs became a dagger.*

> *Stab my breast several times with a dagger,*
> *Open in my heart several doors of delight!*

ABOVE Persian noblemen's daggers, though decorative, were also used to settle feuds. This detail from the 14th-century *Jami al-tawarikh*, a history of 13th-century Persia, shows the murder of a nobleman.

Others equate daggers and the wounds they can inflict with women and love:

*That oppressive mocker holds in her hand the
dagger of vengeance,
In order to shed men's blood, what more does
she hold in her hand?
Draw the dagger and pull the heart from our breast,
So that thou mayest see our heart among the lovers.*

Finally, many inscriptions are much simpler and more straightforward:

Be happy.

The Arabian jambiya

By far the most ubiquitous form of dagger found throughout the Arab world was the jambiya. The name of the weapon is derived from the Persian world *jamb*,

ABOVE The jambiya is still commonly worn in many parts of the Arab world. This young Yemeni man wears his dagger at the waist, tucked into a wide belt as is the usual way in this part of the world.

meaning side. It is often very difficult to distinguish a khanjar from a jambiya and vice versa; indeed, since both terms were used very generally, and meant different things in different parts of the Middle East, as well as in North Africa, India and elsewhere, distinction may be an impossible task. Despite this, writers in English are often tempted to apply general foreign terms to very specific types of weapon, for which they were never intended. The terms *khanjar* and *jambiya* simply mean "dagger". Nevertheless, for the purposes of this book, khanjar is used to refer to the narrower-bladed Indo-Persian daggers which are favoured in the eastern parts of the Muslim world, while jambiya refers in the most generalized terms to the classic "Arabian" dagger that is easily recognized by its wide, steeply curved blade encased in an often highly decorated scabbard that exaggerates the curved form.

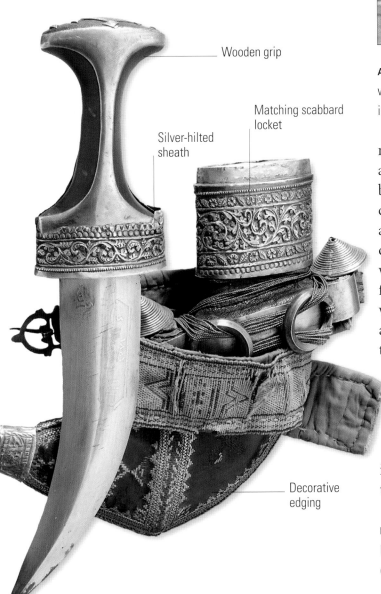

Wooden grip

Matching scabbard locket

Silver-hilted sheath

Decorative edging

LEFT This good-quality Yemeni jambiya was made in around 1900. It retains its original scabbard and belt, with mounts that have been decorated to match the hilt sheath of the dagger.

ABOVE Jambiyas are still manufactured today in very large numbers throughout the Middle East, and are commonly available from local makers and dealers such as this one in Yemen.

The jambiya blade

The arc of the jambiya blade often begins gradually, just forward of the hilt, but increases rapidly in its sweep closer to the point. The blades are often very wide and stiffened by a very proud medial rib. Scabbards usually exaggerate the curved form even further, the scabbard chape often being brought to a full right angle or even turning back up towards the grip.

While both edges of the jambiya blade were sharpened, the inner edge, much like an amputation knife, was kept especially honed. The blades were said to cut easily through the thickest clothes to the bone. The inner edge was used to slash the throat of an enemy, while the curved design made it possible to stab around the opponent's body to strike his back or kidneys. In 1877 an Englishman named John Fryer Keane visited Mecca and described the jambiya as being excellent for cutting through skin and hair, and also stated that it would cut through a rolled-up sheepskin with a single slash.

The hilt is usually a simple waisted affair, having a flat-topped pommel and similarly formed forward section – without any arms or guard – shaped to fit flush with the locket of the scabbard. Hilts are made of wood, bone, ivory or rhinoceros horn. The jambiya

remains an important part of traditional male formal dress in the Middle East, especially in Yemen, Oman and Saudi Arabia. Worn centrally at the waist, the dagger was a prominent fashion statement but was also very quick to draw if the need arose. As jewellery items, jambiya hilts may also be further decorated with gold or silver filagree, amber, coins, coral or semi-precious stones.

Later Persian daggers

Many of the antique Persian daggers on the market today are khanjars dating from the Qajar Period (1781–1925). Most of these are composed of a hilt shaped like a capital "I", carved from either walrus or elephant ivory, joined to a blade having a graceful curve and either a prominent medial rib or central fuller. Normally the blades are made of watered steel. The hilts are usually carved with scenes from Persian history and mythology. A rarer type of khanjar from the Qajar Period features a hilt and scabbard flamboyantly decorated with multicoloured enamel. The cities of Shiraz and Isfahan were both famous centres of fine enamelling: indeed, Isfahani enamellers are still renowned in modern Iran.

Sharp ridged point

The kard

In addition to the curved jambiya and khanjar designs, straight-bladed daggers were also common throughout Persia, Turkey and the wider Middle East. The two most universal forms were the kard and the peshkabz.

Kard simply means "knife" and this term is still used today to refer to an ordinary kitchen knife. The historical weapon does indeed strongly resemble a cooking knife, having a long, usually single-edged, straight blade and a simple grip. Such a weapon, though primarily intended for fighting, would inevitably be used for other purposes. Timurid miniatures show men cutting dough and slitting the throats of sheep with kards.

Some kards make their primary role as a combat weapon more explicit; the points are sometimes specially thickened and shaped like a modern armour-piercing bullet to strengthen them for

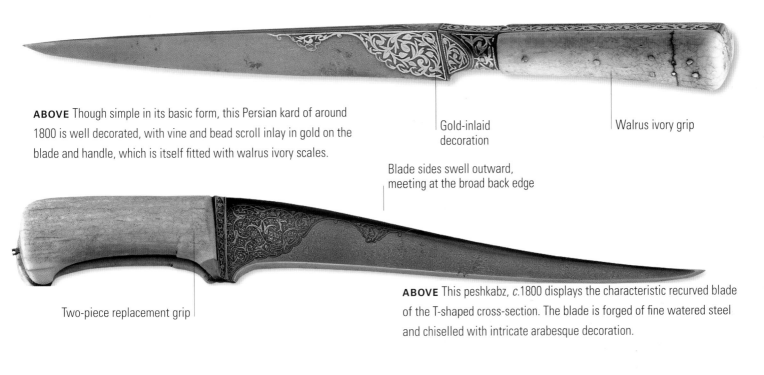

ABOVE Though simple in its basic form, this Persian kard of around 1800 is well decorated, with vine and bead scroll inlay in gold on the blade and handle, which is itself fitted with walrus ivory scales.

Gold-inlaid decoration

Walrus ivory grip

Blade sides swell outward, meeting at the broad back edge

Two-piece replacement grip

ABOVE This peshkabz, *c.*1800 displays the characteristic recurved blade of the T-shaped cross-section. The blade is forged of fine watered steel and chiselled with intricate arabesque decoration.

Chiselled allegorical scene

Carved walrus ivory grip

ABOVE The carved ivory hilts of Persian khanjars of the Qajar Period are very distinctive. The handles feature very fine carved relief work, and are usually fitted with blades of a high quality.

stabbing. These reinforced points were common enough to warrant their own term; in Persian they are fittingly described as *noke makhruti*, a term meaning "cone-point".

Kard grips were frequently made of walrus ivory, although elephant ivory examples are known. Khan Alam, Persian ambassador to the Mughal Court in India during the early 17th century, gave the Emperor Jahangir a dagger with a handle of a special type of walrus ivory speckled with black crystals ("piebald" ivory). The Great Mughal was very impressed and compared the dagger handle to the swirling pattern of watered steel. Horn was another material commonly used for kard grips, as was steel enamelled or decorated with gold overlay.

The peshkabz

The term *peshkabz* originally described the front of a girdle that Persian men wore while wrestling. The use of the same term to describe a dagger then seems

to indicate that a peshkabz was worn centrally, as opposed to the khanjar and the kard, which were tucked to the right and left sides respectively. Of course, multiple knives of these various types were often carried together at the same time

The blade of a peshkabz is easily recognized by its steeply tapered straight or recurved blade, the characteristic feature being its especially thick back. To achieve this thickness while keeping the weight down, the smith would grind down the sides of the blade immediately below the back, so that the back itself could remain 1.5–2mm (.0059–.0078in) wide; the result of this grinding was to give the blade a T-shaped cross-section, rather than the much heavier wedge shape that would otherwise have been the result of the thickening of the back to this extent.

Indian daggers

Daggers from India take many strange and unusual forms. Their variety is a testament to the importance of the elite warrior class for both the Islamic and Hindu traditions. Weapons from the Muslim Mughal Empire, which expanded into northern India in the 16th century, are similar to the Persian weapons from which they are descended, while others, originating in the southern Hindu kingdoms, are unlike anything anywhere else.

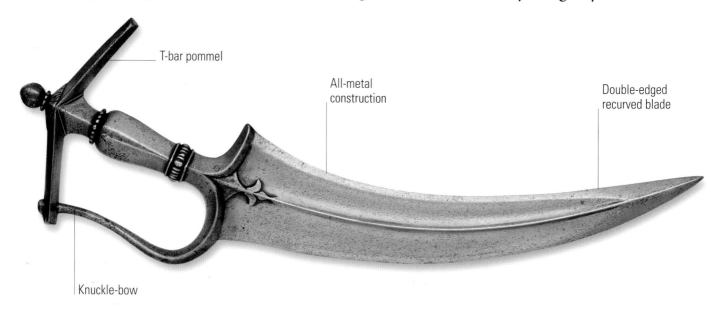

T-bar pommel

All-metal construction

Double-edged recurved blade

Knuckle-bow

India is a vast subcontinent, a place of bewildering variety in art, language and belief. For thousands of years it has been a cultural crossing point, where vast invading empires collided while diverse localized tribes struggled to maintain their lands and unique customs. But even as India's many peoples struggled against each other for territorial and economic supremacy, their many distinctive cultures could not help but influence each other to varying degrees. Thus, for example, did the Muslim Mughals, who were of Persian origin, adopt much from the Hindu and tribal peoples that they conquered in the northern parts of the Indian subcontinent.

The chilanum

One uniquely Indian dagger form is the chilanum. It is characterized by its double-edged recurving blade, usually having a strong central spine and two or more fullers, and by its unusual hilt – the pommel drawn out into a drooping "T", or sometimes curving, frond-like arms. The guard is similarly shaped but with shorter arms, the forward arm often being drawn out to form a knuckle guard. While it has been suggested that the

ABOVE This fine all-steel *chilanum*, made in the south of India in the late 18th century, displays all of the usual features of its type – the drooping T-shaped pommel, knuckle-bow and gently curved blade.

chilanum is Nepalese in origin, it seems to have evolved in the south of India, where it was clearly very common from the 16th century. Sometimes chilanum hilts are carved from hard stone, although most are metal, usually made of steel in one piece with the blade.

Mughal princes were renowned throughout the world for their love of gems and jewels. The finest Mughal chilanums had hilts of pure gold embellished with inlaid precious stones. The chilanum was supposedly introduced to the Mughals by the Rajputs, by way of Emperor Akbar's marriages to Rajput princesses, which brought with them military alliances and a complex intermingling of the Islamic and Hindu cultures. Chilanum blades were invariably of the finest watered steel, and the arms of the guard were worked into plant or animal forms. A famous portrait of Shah Jahan (1592–1666), painted in 1617, shows the Mughal emperor and builder of the Taj Mahal wearing just such a chilanum in his qamarband (waist band).

Wootz steel blades

Some Indian and Persian dagger blades display a beautiful wavy, flowing pattern. This pattern indicates that the blade is made of a high-quality steel generally known today as "wootz". The term perhaps is a derivation or corruption of *ukku*, an old south Indian word for steel.

Possibly as early as the 3rd century BC, centres in south India and Sri Lanka were producing this very high-carbon steel in crucibles; iron and wood charcoal were placed in the crucible, which was heated in a furnace. This produced an iron and carbon alloy – steel. The crucible process causes iron carbide particles to scatter throughout the crystalline structure of the steel. When the steel is tempered through heating and quenching, these particles form into bands. When the steel is lightly etched, by applying a mild acid such as vinegar to its surface, these bands react differently from the steel around them and discolour, producing

RIGHT The mesmerizing patterns of a wootz blade are brought out only when the blade is lightly etched with a weak acid. Over-polishing can easily eradicate the visible pattern.

the extraordinary "watered" pattern. This pattern not only gives the blade an almost magical appearance, it is also a useful indicator of technical quality. This is because patterned blades, having a high carbon content, are very strong and can hold a razor-sharp edge.

The khanjarli

An 18th-century variation of the chilanum is the khanjarli. This dagger may be recognized by its wide, mushroom-like pommel, which supplants the chilanum's T-bar but performs very much the same function: to brace the hand against slippage while dealing overarm blows. Khanjarli pommels and grips are usually made of bone or ivory, two pieces sandwiching the tang and riveted in place. The khanjarli is thought to be Maratha in origin, and is usually associated with Vizianagaram in Orissa, a region famous for its elephants and ivory work. This has led to the suggestion that the distinctive ivory-handled khanjarlis come mainly from this part of India. The Marathas conquered Orissa in the 18th century, and undoubtedly the khanjarli design spread outside of its area of origin in subsequent campaigns.

BELOW Both the chilanum and its cousin the khanjarli were sometimes fitted with recurved blades like this fine example forged in wootz.

Multi-ribbed blade

Wooden hilt

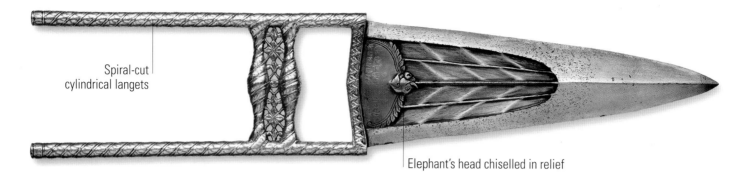

Spiral-cut
cylindrical langets

Elephant's head chiselled in relief

The katar

The most famous Indian dagger is without doubt the katar, or jamdhar. The basic katar is composed of a short, wide blade from the base of which emanate two long, metal langets spaced apart from each other by the width of the user's hand. Between the langets is placed a pair of bars that form the grip of the weapon. So unlike most conventional daggers, which when held project their blades along a line approximately 90 degrees to that of the user's forearm, the katar places the blade in line with the arm, so that the striking action is essentially the same as a punch. Therefore, when striking correctly the user is able to put the whole weight of his body behind his dagger blows. Because the force of katar strikes could be so great, many examples have specially thickened points, to help prevent them bending or breaking. These points may also have improved the katar as an armour-piercing weapon, with which the user could literally punch through the textile, mail and perhaps even plate armour of his opponents on the battlefield.

One Indian fighting style, in evidence from the 16th century onwards, involved two katars, one held in each hand. With each fist armed with a lethal 1ft (30cm) or more of razor-sharp steel, the Indian warrior must have adopted a technique not unlike that of the pugilist, punching at the head and body of his opponent with sudden, lightning-fast attacks.

The katar seems to be of south Indian origin, earliest forms being closely associated with the Vijayanagara Kingdom, a south Indian empire in the Deccan founded in the 14th century. One of the most famous groups of these daggers came from the armoury at Thanjavur, which, with the armoury's

ABOVE This Rajasthani katar of about 1850 carries a typically heavy blade, thickened at the point and ideally suited to stabbing through the light armour typically worn in northwestern India.

dissipation in the late 19th century, has today come to be spread throughout many different museum collections. These early katars generally include a leaf or shell-like plate that protects the back of the hand, usually elaborately decorated with piercing and file-work.

Towards the end of the 16th and into the 17th century, European blades began to be imported into India in very large numbers and many katars dating from the late 1500s and early 1600s are fitted with such blades, which are often broken sword blades. By the second half of the 17th century the more enveloping hand guard was beginning to be discarded in favour of the simpler hilt that is now familiar as the classic katar form.

Stout, straight katar blades are common, but they are by no means the only type. Regional tastes led to a profusion of flamboyant katar designs. While the straight-bladed versions tended to be fashionable in the north of India, wavy or curved blades seemed more popular in the south. Multi-bladed weapons with two or even three blades were not uncommon. Other katars, sometimes referred to as "scissors" katars, were cleverly constructed so that when the grips were squeezed together, the blade split into three, rather like the European sword-catching parrying daggers of the late 16th and 17th centuries. Perhaps the most novel variation

LEFT Like most combination weapons, the effectiveness of pistol katars like this c.1850 weapon is uncertain. The 9.5mm calibre pistols were fired by triggers pulled by the index and little fingers.

RIGHT Mughal miniatures provide vital evidence for the way weapons were worn by noblemen in India. Here a high-ranking boy wears a *katar* in his sash, prominently displayed and close to hand if needed.

on the katar theme was a Rajasthani type that was fitted with two very small flintlock or percussion pistols, one flanking each edge of the blade. The triggers were fitted inwards over the grip, which meant that they could be pulled by the index and little fingers, one at a time or simultaneously. Multiple katars are also known in which one or two smaller katars fit inside a larger one constructed as a sort of sleeve.

Katars were also important status symbols and many survive with extraordinarily varied forms of decoration. Hilts covered in enamel, gems and gold koftgari, blades chiselled with complex figures, scenes and abstract ornament, and sheaths covered in rich silk or velvet were the prize possessions of, for example, the famous Rajput warriors of northwest India. Many Rajput and Mughal princes and noblemen were portrayed with their katars tucked away safely at their waists, ready at all times if needed for self-defence but also an obvious sign of wealth and position. Katars were even used by the Mughal nobility to hunt tigers. Employed in pairs, one katar in each hand, this was without doubt the most impressive but also most hazardous of hunting practices.

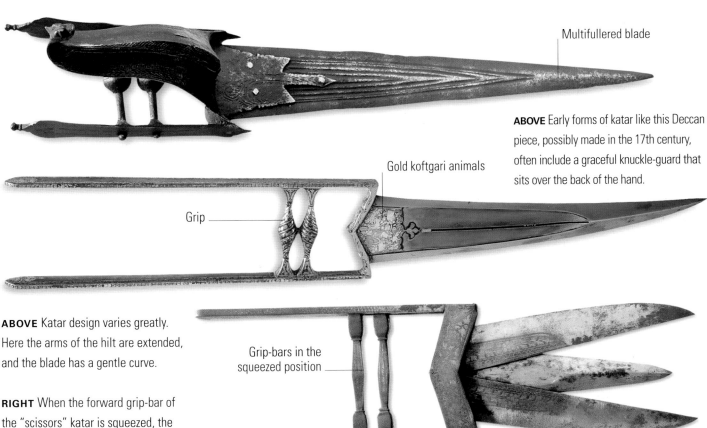

Multifullered blade

ABOVE Early forms of katar like this Deccan piece, possibly made in the 17th century, often include a graceful knuckle-guard that sits over the back of the hand.

Gold koftgari animals

Grip

ABOVE Katar design varies greatly. Here the arms of the hilt are extended, and the blade has a gentle curve.

Grip-bars in the squeezed position

RIGHT When the forward grip-bar of the "scissors" katar is squeezed, the blade spreads apart into three.

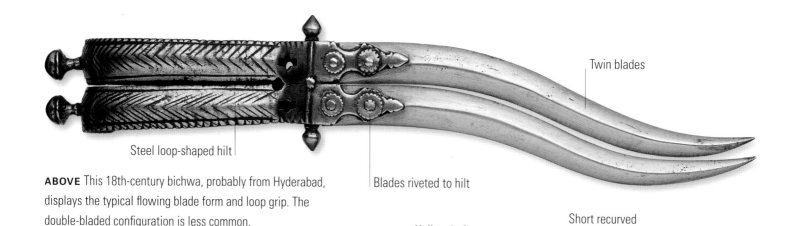

Twin blades

Steel loop-shaped hilt

Blades riveted to hilt

ABOVE This 18th-century bichwa, probably from Hyderabad, displays the typical flowing blade form and loop grip. The double-bladed configuration is less common.

The bichwa and bhuj

Two other distinctively Indian dagger types are the *bichwa*, or "scorpion" dagger, and the *bhuj*, or "elephant" dagger. The bichwa usually has a simple all-metal hilt, having a knuckle guard but no other distinctive features, and a recurved blade, but one much narrower than that found on most chilanums and khanjarlis. Like the latter, the bichwa is probably a Maratha design. This small dagger was easily hidden up a sleeve or in the qamarband, and was especially useful as a weapon for clandestine attack. It is perhaps most famous as the concealed weapon of the famous Maratha war-leader Shivaji (1630–1680), whose Robin Hood-like adventures are still told in the form of stories, poems and films. Shivaji is said to have had a bichwa named *Bhavani* ("giver of life"), which he used (although some accounts insist he used a *bagh-nakh*, or "tiger-claw") to disembowel Afzal Khan, a general in the service of the Mughal Emperor Aurangzeb (1618–1707), who tried to assassinate him during a supposedly friendly meeting.

BELOW This Mughal khanjar is mounted with a classic horsehead grip of jade inlaid with gold. The blade is probably Persian, indicated by the palmette ornament at the ricasso and the recessed panels of the blade.

Hollow haft

Short recurved blade

Stiletto hidden in haft

Scabbard

ABOVE The bhuj represents one of the most unorthodox dagger designs. The elegant dagger blade is mounted at a right angle to a short metal haft. The haft is usually hollow, inside which is often hidden another dagger of more conventional form, a short spike mounted onto the underside of the screw-threaded pommel.

The bhuj takes its name from the city in the Kachchh district of Gujarat (in the extreme west of India) where it was supposedly invented. It is sometimes also referred to as a *gandasa*, or "axe-knife", and is made up of a short, very heavy dagger blade that surmounts a short, axe-like haft (handle). The head of an elephant in profile is very often worked into the metal forming the base of the blade, hence the further nickname "elephant" dagger. Sometimes a small stiletto-like dagger is hidden in the haft of the bhuj, the butt cap of which unscrews to release it.

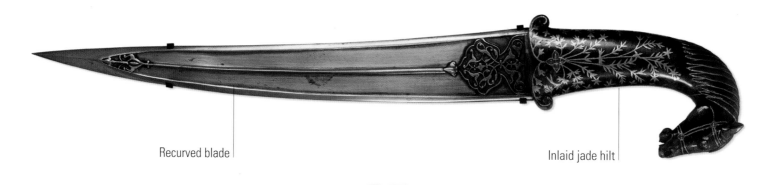

Recurved blade

Inlaid jade hilt

Koftgari decoration

One of the most popular techniques used for the decoration of fine daggers in India was koftgari, a particular type of gold inlay. The origin of the term is a brilliant evocation of the process; the Persian word *koft* means "interwoven", while a *gar* was a goldsmith or gold-beater.

The koftgari process starts with a piece of steel being cross-hatched with hundreds of tiny scratches, made with a special stout knife. Minute strands of gold wire are then worked into the surface, and are held there because the soft gold is pushed down into the scratches, becoming in a way interwoven with the steel.

This process was used to create all sorts of intricate designs, from simple plant forms and geometric patterns to complex scenes including gardens, buildings, trees and animals.

ABOVE The very elegant koftgari work on this Indian katar, which dates from the early 19th century, includes representations of cheetahs, water buffalo and lions.

LEFT Fine weapons made in Lucknow in northern India, such as this 19th-century peshkabz, usually include silver hilts embellished with brightly coloured enamelling.

The Persian influence

While the katar and chilanum originated in the south, the bhuj from the far west, and the khanjarli from the east, other dagger types were introduced from the north. The khanjar was perhaps one of the commonest forms throughout Indo-Persia, popular in Mughal India and Afghanistan but also within the rest of the Islamic world. It is probably of Persian origin, brought to India in the 15th century with the conquest of the first Mughal Emperor. The khanjar's most recognizable attribute is its supremely graceful recurved blade, often with a thickened reinforced stabbing point. Indian khanjar hilts, like those of the Middle East, lack a guard and are usually carved from a single piece of ivory, jade, agate or similar hard stone. Some especially fine examples are made of clear rock-crystal. The handles are often inlaid with precious and semi-precious stones and gold, and commonly carved into horses', rams' and tigers' heads. In depictions of Mughal noblemen these distinctive handles are often seen protruding from their sashes.

Some dagger forms were popular throughout India, but others were only found close to their areas of introduction. The peshkabz and the kard were Persian in origin, introduced by the Mughals. The peshkabz was never adopted with any regularity beyond the north. The kard caught on to some extent in central India, but remained perhaps less common as a fighting weapon. It was common throughout Rajasthan and down into central India, carried along, undoubtedly, by the progress of the Mughal Empire's incursions from the north.

The kris of South-east Asia

Most weapons are something more than a killing tool. They are symbols of status, signifiers of wealth and prestige, or badges of allegiance. But rarely are they believed to possess genuine supernatural powers and seldom is their physical appearance so conducive to such beliefs. The other-worldly appearance of the kris, and the mystical belief system that surrounds it, has promoted a unique relationship between the weapon and its world.

From the 1st century AD onwards, trade routes expanded east from India into Assam, Burma, Indonesia and Malaysia. With the accompanying migrations came also cultural and religious transmission. Hinduism became the dominant faith in some areas of the Malay Peninsula and Archipelago, while Islam and Buddhism prevailed in others. The major faiths intermingled with a bewildering variety of indigenous belief systems practised by many diverse ethnic groups, and so it is not surprising that the weapons found in this vast area are equally multifarious. Indian, Chinese and European influences combined with unique local styles and designs, creating a vast range of edged weapons.

ABOVE A fine kris blade must be mounted with a hilt of equal quality. This example has been intricately carved in a highly individual and complex manner using very diverse materials.

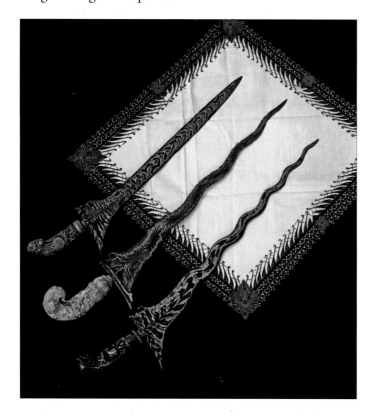

ABOVE The belief in the magical power of the kris is not difficult to understand when one sees a kris blade of exceptional quality, such as these Javanese examples, rippling with swirling colour.

The origins of the kris

This vibrant set of ethnic communities – where many belief systems existed side by side – might not seem like the most obvious environment for a single iconic weapon to evolve. After all, as we have seen, cultural diversity in India generated a great variety of weapons forms and designs. Yet one form of dagger did indeed rise above the many other types of knife and sword in use throughout the Malay Archipelago. The kris, or keris, achieved a cultural status unique in the world history of daggers. It was this weapon, thought to have originated in Java, that later spread throughout southeast Asia – perhaps the only weapon whose use was shared by the many peoples of that region.

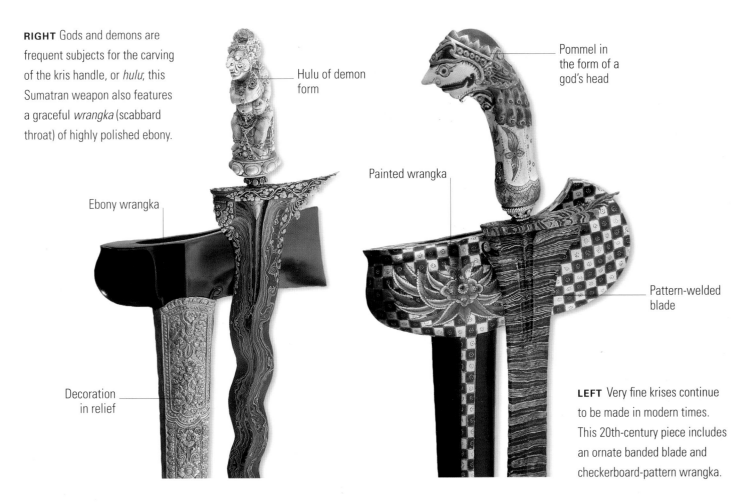

RIGHT Gods and demons are frequent subjects for the carving of the kris handle, or *hulu*; this Sumatran weapon also features a graceful *wrangka* (scabbard throat) of highly polished ebony.

Hulu of demon form

Ebony wrangka

Decoration in relief

Pommel in the form of a god's head

Painted wrangka

Pattern-welded blade

LEFT Very fine krises continue to be made in modern times. This 20th-century piece includes an ornate banded blade and checkerboard-pattern wrangka.

It has been suggested that the kris was inspired by the stingray's stinger, while other theories relate it to the ancient Chinese ko, or dagger-axe, which, like the kris, projects its blade at a right angle to the user's grip. Whatever the origin, it seems clear that the kris had defined itself as a distinctive Malay weapon by the 14th century. A carving at the mid-14th-century Hindu temple of Candi Sukuh in Java depicts a god forging a kris, while one of the earliest known examples bears a date corresponding to AD1342.

The kris blade

This knife is characterized by its long, narrow blade, which can be either straight or, more famously, wavy. Kris blades are pattern-welded works of art, made of up to seven types of iron (meteoric iron being highly prized) and steel braided and forged together. After being formed, the kris blade was carefully ground, polished, boiled in a potion of water, sulphur and salt, and rubbed with lime juice. These processes brought out the blade's welded pattern; not only did the different metals darken and discolour to different degrees, the citric acid also ate into them in varying amounts. Thus the pattern, or *pamor*, of the blade took on a striking, three-dimensional quality, like tiny

meandering canyons and rivers. Malay smiths created around 150 different pamors, each being given a poetically evocative name, such as "tender coconut leaf", "spray of jasmine", "venerable serpent", "flowering of nutmeg", "snakeskin" and "rind of the watermelon".

Although kris forms vary enormously, most blades flare out at the base to form a pointed projection sometimes called the "elephant's trunk". They are fitted with a narrow metal band forming the *ganja*, or guard. A thin tang is forged out of the ganja and inserted into the *ukiran*, or handle, and secured with a gummy paste. The ukiran of the kris is usually a work of art in itself. Beautifully sculpted in ivory (elephant, walrus or even mammoth), horn, wood, bone, brass, silver or gold, kris handles take many forms. Hindu gods and demons, animals, scrollwork, phallic symbols and a number of basic ergonomic forms are all common.

In combat the kris was predominantly a thrusting weapon. The position and shape of the grip, not unlike that of a pistol, allowed the blade to project along the same line as the forearm. Like the Indian katar, it was not uncommon for two krises to be used in combat, one in each hand. The distinctive sheath could also be used to block an opponent's blows.

Foreign interest

Since westerners first became aware of the kris, it has been a source of fascination and curiosity. Sir Francis Drake (*c.*1540–1596) brought krises back to England from Java in 1580, while another was sent to King James I (1566–1625) as a gift in 1612. They also became popular with European artists in the 16th and 17th centuries. Rembrandt (1606–1669), for example, included krises in several of his works. He grasps one in an engraved and etched self-portrait (mistakenly titled *Self-Portrait with Raised Sabre*), while a soldier plunges another into Samson's eye in *The Blinding of Samson*.

A magical relationship

A kris was, for its owner, an intensely personal object. It was washed and anointed during annual rituals, during which offerings were also made to it, in similar fashion to the sword worship practised by some Indian Hindus. A kris was considered one of a man's basic possessions, along with a house, a wife and a horse. It asserted a man's identity and associations, both within his family and in society in general. A kris passed down through a family was a tangible bond between a man and his ancestors, a link between the living and the dead. In Java the relationship between a kris and its owner was so strong that the weapon could actually stand in for a bridegroom at his wedding if for some reason he was unable to be present himself.

The kris was also believed to possess many mystical properties. Some have been said to fly out of their sheaths at night to kill unsuspecting victims. Others were thought to have healing powers. One of the most widely held ideas was that a kris could kill someone just by being pointed at them; great care was therefore taken in the handling of a kris to prevent accidental harm caused by someone inadvertently coming in line with the point. In Bali, specially designed kris stands in the form of animals or demons held the weapon vertically to minimize the danger from its projected magical energy. It is also said that the very best krises can kill simply by being driven into the footprint, shadow or a photo of the intended victim.

An ancient weapon in a modern world

Krises featured in Indonesian warfare into the 20th century. During the Philippines Campaign (1899–1905), local kris-wielding warriors mounted many ambushes and nocturnal attacks against the American military. In 1903, the US Army fought a group of Moros near Jolo that included 4000 men armed with krises.

Their leader was later captured, but the American force guarding him was in turn ambushed by men with krises; he was rescued and a number of the Americans killed or injured, including the commander, whose hand was so badly slashed that several of his fingers had to be amputated.

Since the 1960s, the kris has begun to lose much of its cultural and religious influence in Indonesian society. Although a small number of master smiths practising the traditional art form can still be found, they are now very few. Transmission of the skill of kris making has also been made difficult as the younger generation becomes increasingly westernized.

Efforts from the 1990s onwards have, however, revived the craft of kris making to some extent, and in 2005 UNESCO heralded the kris a Masterpiece of the Oral and Intangible Heritage of Humanity (Third Proclamation).

RIGHT This drawing made in 1864 gives some idea of what an Indonesian (Javanese) warband might have looked like. The leading warrior holds his kris, signifying his elite status, high in the air.

ABOVE Another kris appears in Rembrandt's *The Blinding of Samson* (1636); here a soldier plunges one into Samson's eye. It was undoubtedly thought to be suitably exotic and thus appropriate to the Biblical theme.

The Japanese tanto

Unlike the many different dagger forms that evolved elsewhere in Asia, those of Japan remained remarkably consistent in design throughout their long history. A short, single-edged, thick-backed blade, ground to a steep wedge shape in cross-section, remained the sidearm of samurai warriors for several hundred years. In that time the design changed very little, remaining essentially a miniature version of the swords with which it was partnered.

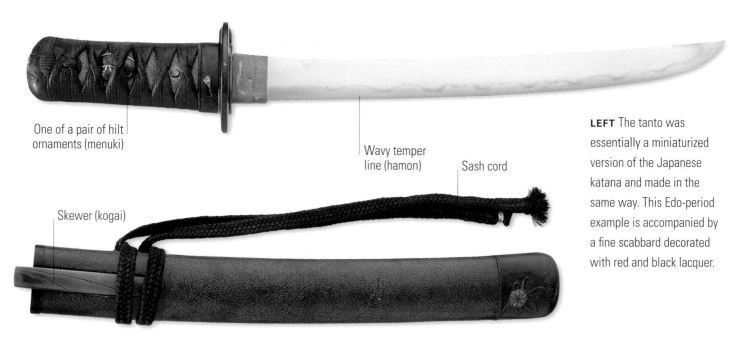

One of a pair of hilt ornaments (menuki)

Skewer (kogai)

Wavy temper line (hamon)

Sash cord

LEFT The tanto was essentially a miniaturized version of the Japanese katana and made in the same way. This Edo-period example is accompanied by a fine scabbard decorated with red and black lacquer.

The distinctive Japanese dagger, the tanto, is thought to have first appeared in the pre-medieval Heian Period (AD794–1185). Early tantos seem to have been very basic utilitarian implements, unworthy of note. It was not until the very end of that era that the tanto distinguished itself, as a work of art as well as a weapon, during the bloody Gempei War (1180–85) fought between the rival Minamoto and Taira clans.

By this time the warrior culture of the samurai had fully developed, and along with it, codified systems of combat. Warriors of the late Heian Period carried the bow, a long-bladed staff weapon called a naginata and the long sword, or tachi, as their primary weapons, along with the tanto as a weapon of last resort. These weapons, and the sequence of their use, are vividly described in an account of the first Battle of Uji (1180), the opening battle of the Gempei War. One passage from the epic *Tale of the Heike* (1371), as follows, relates how the warrior Tsutsui Jomyo Meishu fought the Taira samurai on the Uji bridge itself, in an attempt to prevent them crossing and destroying the fleeing Minamoto forces:

And loosing off twenty arrows like lightning flashes he slew twelve of the Taira samurai and wounded eleven more … throwing away his bow … With his naginata he cut down five of the enemy but with the sixth the blade snapped … he drew his tachi … and cut down eight men. But as he brought down the ninth with an exceedingly mighty blow on the helmet, the blade broke at the hilt …. Then seizing his dagger, which was the only weapon he had left, he plied it as one in a death fury.

The tanto and ritual suicide

This dagger was not only the samurai's final option in hand-to-hand combat. It was also the weapon with which he killed himself when defeated in battle or dishonoured. After the destruction of his forces by the Taira at Uji, the Minamoto commander Yorimasa quickly wrote a death poem on the back of his war fan before using his tanto to cut two long slashes into his abdomen. This is the earliest known instance of a samurai committing *seppuku*, or ritual suicide after a battlefield defeat.

A lethal work of art

Following the Gempei War and throughout the subsequent Kamakura Period (1186–1333), which marks the beginning of the Middle Ages in Japan, the tanto developed into a weapon pleasing to the eye and worthy of respect, as skilfully made and as beautifully decorated as any sword. The blade was constructed in the same way as that of the sword; it was single-edged and strong-backed, 15–30cm (6–12in) long, with an asymmetric point tapering diagonally to the back.

Early forms of the dagger were also termed *koshi-gatana*, or "loin-sword" and were worn tucked into the armoured samurai's sash, or *uwa-obi*. While the

ABOVE This dramatic detail from an early 17th-century version of the Kamakura/Muromachi *gunki-mono* ("war-tales") shows the monk Mongaku attacking a samurai with a *tanto*.

earliest forms had curved blades, by the Muromachi Period (1334–1572) nearly straight blades became more common. The dagger's companion, the sword, was also changing; the long tachi was increasingly being replaced by the shorter, handier katana. The katana was not slung like the tachi but thrust through the girdle along with the dagger. The mounts of these early sword and dagger sets often did not match, although later they would be decorated as a pair.

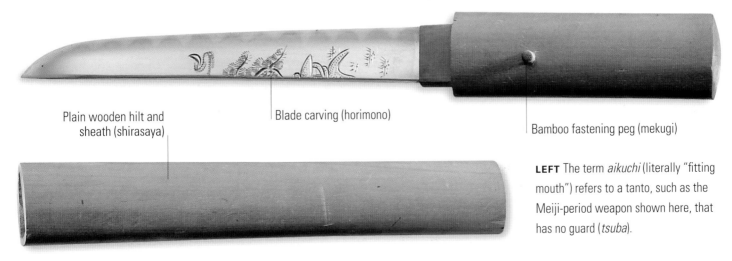

Plain wooden hilt and sheath (shirasaya)

Blade carving (horimono)

Bamboo fastening peg (mekugi)

LEFT The term *aikuchi* (literally "fitting mouth") refers to a tanto, such as the Meiji-period weapon shown here, that has no guard (*tsuba*).

LEFT The Japanese samurai, like the western knight, was armed with a number of different weapons. In addition to a powerful bow and sharp arrows, he also carried a long sword (tachi) and short sword (tanto).

desperate sacrifice was later held up as a powerful example of samurai honour and loyalty; the bloodstained floorboards from the room where the women and children died were later built into the ceiling of a nearby temple.

The decline of the tanto

The tanto was gradually being replaced as the companion weapon of the sword during the violent Momayama Period (1573–1603). The Edo (or Tokugawa) Period (1603–1867) that followed began with the unification of Japan under Tokugawa Ieyasu (1543–1616) and ushered in over 250 years of cultural development and relative peace. The tanto fell quickly out of use as the symbolism of weapons became as important as their application. Although the production of the more symbolic elements of the samurai's dress, namely his armour and sword, continued, the making of the tanto fell dramatically, and most of those made were imitations of the daggers of previous eras.

In 1868 the Medieval Period in Japan officially came to an end with the Meiji Restoration, which ended the rule of the Tokugawa shoguns and established a new line of imperial rulers. Members of the Imperial Court adopted ancient, pre-shogunate fashions, including the wearing of the tachi and tanto. Many daggers were produced before World War II, but Japan's defeat in 1945 and subsequent weapons ban meant that they ceased being made once again.

The kaiken

Noblewomen used a smaller version of the tanto called a kaiken to commit suicide with a swift thrust to the throat, especially in cases where the castle of their lord was taken by storm. In the Siege of Fushimi in 1596, the entire family of the castle's lord, Torii Mototada, killed themselves to avoid capture when this great fortress – near Kyoto – fell after a great battle. This

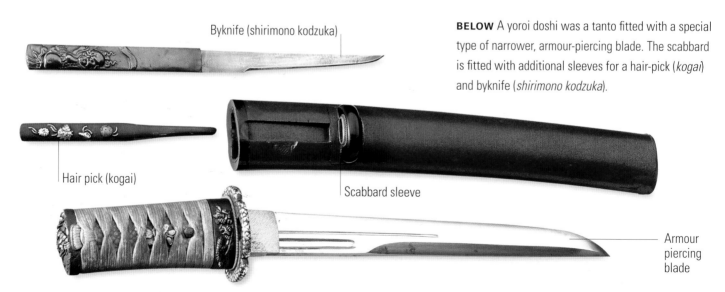

Byknife (shirimono kodzuka)

Hair pick (kogai)

Scabbard sleeve

Armour piercing blade

BELOW A yoroi doshi was a tanto fitted with a special type of narrower, armour-piercing blade. The scabbard is fitted with additional sleeves for a hair-pick (*kogai*) and byknife (*shirimono kodzuka*).

Seppuku

As *bushido* – the Japanese warrior code – developed in the 12th and 13th centuries, seppuku quickly became one of its central elements. Unlike the European code of chivalry, which required defeated and captured knights to be compassionately treated, bushido advocated contempt for one's defeated enemies; if taken prisoner, a samurai was tortured and killed. Seppuku initially evolved as an honourable way for warriors to avoid capture after defeat in battle, but later became a way to salvage and even increase one's honour in recompense for some disreputable or disgraceful act. It was also adopted as a more respectable alternative to execution granted to condemned samurai.

Seppuku provided perhaps the most iconic role for the dagger in Japan. It involved the seated samurai taking up his tanto and plunging it into the left side of his own abdomen. He then calmly cut a long slash across his stomach. The bravest samurai would sometimes attempt a second cut, either another horizontal slash or an even more excruciating vertical cut, before expiring in agony.

As late as the 1860s, Algernon Bertram Freeman-Mitford, the British ambassador to Japan, described in his book *Tales of Old Japan* a seppuku ritual witnessed by a colleague:

The case of a young fellow, only twenty years old, of the Choshiu clan, which was told me the other day by an eye-witness, deserves mention as a marvellous instance of determination. Not content with giving himself the one necessary cut, he slashed himself thrice horizontally and twice vertically. Then he stabbed himself in the throat until the dirk protruded on the other side, with its sharp edge to the front; setting his teeth in one supreme effort, he drove the knife forward with both hands through his throat, and fell dead.

BELOW This fabricated seppuku ritual was staged in about 1875. Two samurai act as witnesses while another acts as headsman.

The modern era

Today, knives, daggers and bayonets are found all over the world. Although the role of a separate fighting knife has diminished, the bayonet remains standard issue to every infantryman serving in a professional army. At the same time, fine-quality edged weapons have gained respect as an art form. Created by modern smiths drawing on 6000 years of experience, these art-object weapons are at once traditional and highly contemporary.

Outside the military world, specialist fighting knives are still produced for the purposes of self-defence, and the demand for survival knives and multi-use "sportsmen's" knives is as strong as ever. Additionally, many people around the world collect historic edged weapons, as much for their craftsmanship as their history. This concept of knives as objects of creative design as well as utility is a growing trend among many modern bladesmiths, especially in the United States.

The art of the knife

Craftsmen today have the huge advantage in their work not only of exact temperature and time control but also the knowledge of precisely why different metals behave the way they do, and exactly how their properties may be manipulated to produce a very wide range of forms and varying effects. Heat and chemical processes, for example, can now be used to create an extraordinary range of colours in steel, giving visual qualities to modern knives that were never possible before. A seemingly endless array of materials are at the disposal of the modern craftsman,

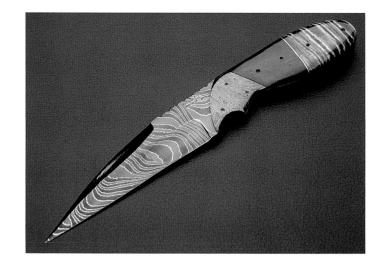

ABOVE Dated 2005, the etched, heat-tinted blade, crucible steel bolsters and handle made of blackwood burl and fossilized mammoth tooth of this fine specimen demonstrate the creativity of modern smiths, such as P.J. Ernest.

BELOW Richard Furrer's "Palm-leaf Bowie" combines a Javanese *Blarka Ngirdi* ("Palm-Leaf") pamor, typical Bowie "Spanish notch" and a Japanese-style *mokume-gane* wood-grain metal guard. The handle is a 30,000-year-old Walrus tusk.

Polished wood scabbard

Walrus-ivory handle

Bowie-style Spanish notch

"Palm leaf" pamor blade pattern

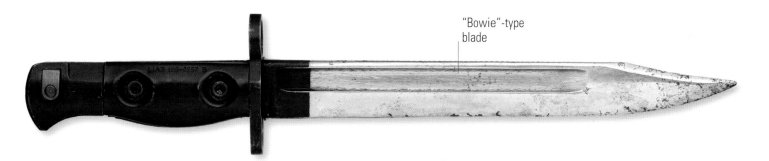

"Bowie"-type blade

ABOVE The L1A3 knife bayonet for the British 7.62mm SLR was introduced in 1959 and remained in use for nearly 30 years. It was used with legendary effectiveness in the Falklands War.

not only modern or rare metals such as titanium, meteoric iron, and many forms of exotic watered steels, but also more unusual organic materials and minerals such as fossilized mammoth and mastodon ivory, hematite and tanzanite.

The modern bayonet

With advances in automatic weapons, one could easily assume that the bayonet would quickly become obsolete. However, bayonets are still issued to infantrymen in most modern armies. How could such an apparently outdated weapon as the bayonet, devised more than 400 years ago, continue to demand a special place in the soldier's arsenal?

The bayonet's functions in present-day war zones are diverse. Despite the increasing effectiveness of firearms in close combat, the bayonet remains an important alternative. In the Vietnam War, US Marines and the North Vietnamese Army fought each other with fixed bayonets at the Siege of Khe Sanh (30 March 1968). At the Battle of Mount Tumbledown (13–14 June 1982) during the Falklands War, British troops stormed Argentinean positions with fixed bayonets in a famous night attack. More recently, in the Second Gulf (Iraq) War (2003–), soldiers from the Argyll and Sutherland Highlanders regiment of the British Army executed a bayonet charge against members of a Shi'ite militia who had ambushed them near the city of Amara (reported 15 May 2004).

The bayonet was not an uncommon sight during both Iraq wars. In the unpredictable environment of urban warfare, especially when clearing buildings or bunkers, an attack at close quarters is always a danger and a fixed bayonet a

Wire-cutting tool

Scabbard

ABOVE The old desire to design a bayonet that serves more than one function continues today; this knife bayonet for the British SA-80 assault rifle is also intended to convert for use as a wire-cutter.

sensible precaution. The bayonet obviously becomes more important to a soldier who runs out of ammunition, but it can also prove a decisive weapon in the face of a surprise attack during reloading, or similar circumstances. Yet perhaps just as important as its practical fighting applications are the psychological advantages: the inexperienced soldier may feel more confident entering battle at close quarters with his bayonet in place; the fierce aspect of the edged weapon is just as strong today as it ever was. It serves to embolden the wielder and often terrifies the enemy. It also gives the modern soldier the sense that he is a part of a martial tradition and in possession of an ancient warrior skill that makes him better than his ill-disciplined opponent. These are advantages that cannot be overcome by technological change. At least, not yet.

Index

ABOVE 17th-century Indian khanjar
with decorated blade and Mughal hilt.